BLACKPINK

BLACKPINK

K-POP'S NO. 1 GIRL GROUP

ADRIAN BESLEY

Michael O'Mara Books Limited

First published in Great Britain in 2019 by
Michael O'Mara Books Limited
9 Lion Yard
Tremadoc Road
London SW4 7NQ

A CIP catalogue record for this book is available from the British Library.

Papers used by Michael O'Mara Books Limited are natural, recyclable products made
from wood grown in sustainable forests. The manufacturing processes conform to the
environmental regulations of the country of origin.

ISBN: 978-1-78929-192-6 in paperback print format
ISBN: 978-1-78929-193-3 in ebook format

1 2 3 4 5 6 7 8 9 10
Cover design by Barbara Ward
Designed and typeset by Claire Cater
Front cover image: Roger Kisby/Getty Images for YouTube
Back cover image: Christopher Polk/Shutterstock
Printed and bound by CPI Group (UK) Ltd, Croydon, CR0 4YY
www.mombooks.com

MIX
Paper from
responsible sources
FSC® C020471
FSC
www.fsc.org

CONTENTS

INTRODUCTION

Perhaps you were an early Blackpink fan who eagerly anticipated the release of 'Boombayah' and 'Whistle'? Maybe it was the hit 'Ddu-du Ddu-du', the Dua Lipa collaboration 'Kiss and Make Up' or the group's triumphant Coachella 2019 performance that piqued your interest? Whenever you stumbled on this K-pop phenomenon, though, there is so much to discover or relive in this story of four of the most enchanting and talented figures in pop music.

This book is for Blinks (followers of Blackpink), new fans and those curious about how a group from a small country in Asia conquered the world. It tells of how Blackpink was formed, traces their journey to global superstardom, details the personal stories of each of the members and – for those new to K-pop – explains how the traits, customs and culture of this sensation have fuelled the group's success.

It might seem strange to find a biography of a group who have been around for only three years and recorded only a dozen or so hits. What can there be to say? It turns out there is an amazing amount, because these four girls – Jisoo, Jennie, Rosé and Lisa – are special. They have packed more into their (so-far) short career than many pop groups manage in decades. They have made history, broken records, travelled the world performing sell-out concerts and created some of the catchiest bops of recent times.

Anyone who goes beyond listening to their hits and delves deeper into the group will find themselves presented with some puzzling questions … Why is an entertainment company so important? What is girl crush? How come not all these K-pop stars are actually from Korea? And what do they do when they are not on stage? The answers to all of these and other conundrums reveal just who Blackpink are and what makes them tick.

It is clear from any photo of the group – whether they are on stage, at a photoshoot or out in public – that they are four extraordinarily beautiful women. But their undoubted beauty is just a small part of their success and the pictures can't tell the story of how they have developed their personal style on and off stage, of their individual charisma and charm, of their immense talent as singers, rappers and dancers, and of the sheer hard work they have put in to earn the success they have today. That's what this book does!

These girls were not born with a silver microphone at their mouths. Jisoo, Jennie, Rosé and Lisa have trained to be pop stars – or 'idols', as they're called in K-pop – since they were young teenagers. They came from Australia and Thailand as well as South Korea and were selected ahead of thousands of hopefuls at auditions to live in a dormitory in Seoul, where they spent between four and six years working exhaustively on their performance skills. Even then, they never knew if they would be selected by their company to be in a group or ultimately be rejected, which is what happens to so many trainees.

Those within the entertainment company have talked about how this group practically picked itself. These four young girls were incredibly hardworking and talented, but perhaps more importantly they had developed a fabulous bond with each other.

Far from home, they felt like family, supported one another, helped anyone who was struggling to learn a language or perfect a dance routine, and cheered up those who were feeling homesick. This togetherness would prove vitally important as they faced the triumphs and disappointments of a career in pop music.

The three short years since their debut have seen Blackpink succeed beyond all expectations, as a group and as individuals. Their hits have broken YouTube records and topped charts in dozens of countries. They have performed in massive venues across four continents and each of the members has become a star and a fashion icon, with social-media accounts followed by fellow celebrities and millions of fans.

> Their hits have broken YouTube records and topped charts in dozens of countries.

Many of those fans count themselves as Blinks, whose unconditional devotion to the group has been, and continues to be, vital to their success. They avidly support the group and the members' individual activities, help spread the word about Blackpink, maximize the views on YouTube, ensure they are trending on social media and, of course, raise the roof at concerts. The Blackpink members are fully aware of the love they receive and in turn are always eager to make sure Blinks know the feeling is mutual.

Blinks play an important part in the story of Blackpink; a journey that has transformed four young teenagers into global stars. It is not a tale of overnight success, but one of disappointment, surprise and elation – and one that begins before these idols were even born …

ONE

K-POP AND GIRL CRUSH

These days, most music fans have a sense of what K-pop is. It's pop music from South Korea, an East Asian country bordered by (and at odds with) North Korea and separated by 500 miles of ocean from Japan. The version of K-pop seen most around the world is boy bands and girl groups, often with numerous members. Their songs are usually upbeat and accompanied by complex and synchronized choreography. The members of the groups are seriously beautiful, characterized by their ultra-smooth skin, designer clothes and exquisite make-up. That's certainly all true, but it's also a vast generalization, because actually there are hundreds of incredibly varied K-pop acts.

South Koreans love their pop music. They listen to music from the West (Katy Perry, Sam Smith, Ariana Grande, U2 and others have all played in Seoul over the last few years) and from Japan, but they are most proud of their home-grown acts, which they follow fanatically, with TV shows, newspapers and websites feeding an insatiable appetite. Talent shows are especially popular; TV series such as *Superstar K* or *Produce 101* can receive massive viewing figures.

For a long time, K-pop (known as *gayo* in Korean) was dominated by ballads and trot music, a style characterized by its two-beat background rhythm (trot is short for foxtrot) and a distinctive vocal style. Then, in 1992, a group called Seo Taiji and Boys appeared on a TV talent show performing their single 'Nan Arayo' ('I Know'). They came last in the show, but their single, an innovative fusion of American and Korean pop, would top the country's charts – for seventeen weeks. Seo Taiji and Boys inspired a host of new Korean groups ready to fill their songs with a US-influenced hip-hop style.

The pioneering Seo Taiji and Boys split in 1996, with one of the Boys' rappers, Yang Hyun-suk, setting up his own company (named YG Entertainment) to create, produce and manage K-pop acts. Around the same time and with the same aims, SM Entertainment and JYP Entertainment were formed. The Big Three, as they became known, had the experience, finance and know-how to produce hit after hit, and they have dominated K-pop right up to the present day.

> Seo Taiji and Boys split in 1996, with one of the Boys' rappers, Yang Hyun-suk, setting up his own company (named YG Entertainment) to create, produce and manage K-pop acts.

For over twenty years, K-pop has looked to the West for musical influences, taking in rock, pop and R&B, as well as hip-hop and rap music. This has all been assimilated into a style that has distinctive Korean characteristics. The Korean public demand entertainment; K-pop acts are attractive, colourful and visually interesting. Choreography is a major component, as is vocal performance, whether in upbeat bops or doleful ballads. Despite some recent high-profile scandals, Korea remains a conservative and morally strict country. Songs with references to sex, drugs and alcohol are often banned from radio and TV, and artists are expected to remain charming and innocent at all times.

Korean television is watched by millions and can be key to the success of K-pop acts. Music shows proliferate with *Inkigayo, Show! Music Core, Music Bank, M Countdown, Show Champion* and *The Show* guaranteeing there is a pop programme on TV most days of the week. The fact that the shows usually feature 'live' acts instead of music videos ensures that performance is a prized aspect of K-pop. On-point choreography, stage presence, stunning outfits and good looks are just as essential as the songs and the vocal performances. Acts feature their latest songs and each show awards a weekly trophy based on various permutations of chart position, downloads and viewers' votes.

K-pop artists are also expected to take their place, as a group or individually, alongside comedians, actors and other celebrities on the nation's incredibly popular variety shows, such as *Knowing Bros, Running Man* and *Weekly Idol*. These sometimes involve interviews and performances, but more often focus on amusing challenges that highlight artists' characters, skills and humour. Some groups will also have their own variety or reality shows, which enable fans to get to know the members better.

Having established themselves, K-pop artists eagerly await the awards season that spans the New Year period. There are many ceremonies, but the most prestigious are the Golden Disc Awards, the Melon Music Awards, Mnet Asian Music Awards (MAMA) and the Seoul Music Awards. *Bonsang*s or prizes are given to a number of high-achieving acts, but every artist ultimately craves a *daesang*, the top prize given for the song, artist and album of the year.

K-pop has a name for the stars who thrive in this high-profile world: idols. The Big Three and other smaller entertainment companies are in the business of creating highly talented, charismatic performers who can be successful idols. They will go to great extremes to find, train and develop the singer or dancer they believe can become a star. The process begins with the companies hosting fiercely competitive auditions and scouring talent shows in search of potential idols. The successful young artists, often in their early teens or even younger, are contracted as trainees and live in dormitories with other hopefuls.

The companies might take a vocalist and train them as a rapper or find talented dancers and improve their singing; some members with no special talent apart from exceptionally good looks and stage presence (known as 'visuals') are given singing and dancing lessons to bring them up to scratch. Together, these trainees face a seemingly never-ending boot camp of dancing, singing, exercise, diet regimes and language lessons, frequently while still attending school or college to complete their education. It is an exacting process from which many drop out, finding it too tough to continue, while others are rejected for not reaching the required standards.

The company remains in control, eventually putting their trainees into groups or selecting them as solo artists. They choose the name, image, choreography and songs, quite often with little input from the act. Common to nearly every K-pop group is a leader who acts as the spokesperson for the group, a position usually given to the eldest or the member who spent longest as a trainee. There is also a *maknae*, the group's youngest member, who is like the baby of the family, cute and adorable.

Once the group is selected and settled, the company begins preparing for their debut – the official unveiling of the group. The preparation for this can last months or even a year or more, with debut dates being postponed if the company doesn't think the act is ready. Ahead of the debut, the company works hard to create excitement among the press and public. This includes releasing teaser photographs, videos and sometimes even pre-debut tracks to build interest. To create even more anticipation, one member is often kept secret until the last minute.

> The preparation for [debut] can last months or even a year or more, with debut dates being postponed if the company doesn't think the act is ready.

The debut itself is when the act is first seen together by the public. In order to make a big splash, this is often done with a showcase in front of invited journalists but is also streamed online. Their debut stage, the group's first performance, usually takes place on one of the weekly music shows. It is a nerve-wracking time for the young artists, who know their careers could depend on how well they come across. Online forums will be assessing how good they looked, whether they can sing (sometimes groups, especially those just starting out, mime on TV), if they danced in sync and how they compare to other new groups.

If a new group can negotiate a successful debut and build a fan base, they will have the chance of a comeback. This doesn't mean they remain dormant for a time or even necessarily have a break; it's the term given for their next launch and set of appearances on the weekly shows. Once again previewed and teased beforehand, the comeback often has a new 'concept': a subtle or even a major change in image or sound. For at least a year, the group will be known as a rookie act. This gives them a certain freedom from criticism (K-pop fans can be a tough crowd to please!), but a strong debut will also carry a heavy burden of expectation.

The passion of K-pop fans is an essential element in sustaining a successful act. Interaction with fans through social media and fan meets can quickly garner the most dedicated and loyal support. These fans are sometimes given an official name by the group, have their own forums and can create an incredible atmosphere at concerts. Twice named their fan club Once, BTS have ARMY and, of course, Blackpink have their Blinks! K-pop fans have devised ingenious ways of interacting with their idols. Not content with simple screaming and wild applause (although that happens), they hold up light sticks in the group's colour, sometimes in co-ordinated waves; produce massive banners of support; and perform fan chants over the intros and breaks or as a reply to choruses.

South Korean culture has been growing in global prominence over the past decade – so much so that there is a word for it, *hallyu*, which means 'the Korean Wave'. From TV dramas to cosmetics and especially pop music, South Korean exports have become fashionable and popular across South-East Asia and in many other parts of the world. YouTube and other video channels (especially the livestreaming service V Live) enable fans everywhere to see their idols, while hundreds of forums allow them to keep abreast of news from South Korea and connect with others around the globe.

Many regions with no obvious connection with Korea – notably South America, Australia and the Middle East – have an amazing enthusiasm for K-pop, but it is truly a global phenomenon with fans all around the world. In the West, K-pop has been gradually gaining mainstream attraction, with Psy's 2012 hit 'Gangnam Style' a major breakthrough. The boy bands Big Bang and EXO made inroads into the US Billboard charts, but the post-2017 success of BTS has been unprecedented and has opened the door for other groups.

Blackpink have many of the classic characteristics of K-pop idols. They are part of the YG Entertainment company; all the members were discovered by YG talent scouts and they all spent between four and six years as trainees before eventually debuting. Lisa and Jennie were developed as rappers, while all four spent hundreds of hours practising in the dance studio. The group's stylish, assertive, even provocative image was carefully developed, too, and took another facet of K-pop – girl groups and the emergence of 'girl crush' – another step forward.

Although girl groups had long been a popular feature of Korean entertainment, the first K-pop girl groups emerged in the late 1990s. The trio S.E.S, four-member group Fin.K.L and five-piece Baby V.O.X dominated the airwaves and inspired a plethora of groups known as the 'Second Generation'. Among these, Girls' Generation (whose hit 'Gee' remains an anthem for young Koreans) and Wonder Girls became huge names, releasing hit after hit. Wonder Girls (whose song 'So Hot' was later covered by Blackpink) even came very close to finding success in the USA.

Girl groups traditionally had a cute and innocent image, and often dressed in schoolgirl-style uniforms or candy-coloured wispy dresses, but among the Second Generation were acts who rejected ultra-feminine, bubblegum pop for a more individualist and hard-edged attitude. Miss A, Brown Eyed Girls, f(x) and 4 Minute were among this wave whose feisty style would be labelled

> 2NE1 were one of the most successful K-pop girl groups ever. They sold 66.5 million records and had nine number one hits in South Korea.

'girl crush'. This term was widely applied to any girl group that expressed their individuality or sexuality or even just exuded self-confidence. The breakout year for girl crush was 2010, with hits such as Miss A's 'Bad Girl Good Girl', 4 Minutes' 'Hot Issue' and Brown Eyed Girls' 'Abracadabra'; former cutesy Girls' Generation even took on an edge with their 'Run Devil Run'.

Up to that point, YG Entertainment had not been in the business of girl groups. They had R&B-style singer Seven and hip-hop boy band Big Bang on the label, and they were far too cool for that. The trend for girl crush, however, completely fitted the bill. YG launched 2NE1 in 2009 and these girls – Bom, Dara, Minzy and CL – took the concept and ran with it. They seemed like they wore whatever they wanted, but always looked stylish. Crop tops, minidresses, bomber jackets, swimsuits, rock T-shirts, boots, sneakers – they threw it all together and looked sensational. Although they leaned on black and white, they were never afraid to add bold and vibrant colours into one coherent style in outfits ranging from punk to femme-fatale glam.

A four-member group, their stage presence was unrivalled, with fierce choreography and the trademark YG energy making them stand out. The way their smooth vocals were mixed with powerful rapping brought comparisons with boy-band groups, especially Big Bang, their superstar counterparts at the company with whom they often collaborated. 2NE1 were one of the most successful K-pop girl groups ever. They sold 66.5 million records and had nine number one hits in South Korea – 'I Am the Best', 'Come

Back Home' and 'Take the World On' being among the biggest of them. Internationally they were popular, too, especially across East and South-East Asia. In 2014 they were making inroads in the US, appearing in episodes of *The Bachelor* and *America's Next Top Model*, and their album *Crush* reached number sixty-one on the Billboard 200; at that time, the highest-ever chart position for a K-pop album in the US.

Was it too good to last? In 2015, a scandal involving Bom led to the group going on hiatus with just a final memorable performance at the MAMA awards ceremony for fans to remember them by. Nothing more was heard of them until November 2016, when YG announced the group were disbanding with a farewell single, 'Goodbye'. By then K-pop's Third Generation had arrived on the scene. Girl crush was now an option that girl groups such as Red Velvet, Twice and Mamamoo could use in their concepts, with even a cutesy group like Apink happy to go edgy. YG Entertainment, however, believed no one could do girl crush quite like them. They had primed a girl group that could take the concept and make it relevant and modern for today's teens and twenty-somethings. They had a group to take on 2NE1's mantle. They had Blackpink.

Just like their seniors, Blackpink not only had a girl-crush image but also had four members, were all around twenty years old on debut, had songs written and produced by Teddy Park, and had members who had grown up outside Korea. No wonder many onlookers immediately dismissed them as 2NE1 clones. Who were these girls? And were they special enough to shine in their own right?

TWO

PINK PUNK
THE EVOLUTION OF BLACKPINK

In 2011 YG were riding high. In Big Bang and 2NE1 they had two of the biggest names in K-pop and their success had helped the label get listed on South Korea's KOSDAQ stock market. YG were now up there with Samsung, Hyundai and other massive companies. They had to talk the talk and walk the walk, and they needed big plans to attract potential shareholders.

Stocks and shares are probably the least glamorous words to appear in the Blackpink story, but they mark the very beginning of the group. At a press conference on 8 November 2011 YG's head honchos sketched out the company's ambitions. YG had always had a 'family' feel: it had limited numbers of trainees and acts and concentrated on the Korean market, they explained. Now, the company would be expanding – not only in developing talent, but in appealing to a global audience, too. YG had over thirty trainees and were preparing three idol groups, one of which was a female group, made up of trainees all under the age of twenty, who were scheduled for debut in the early half of 2012. It was that last piece of information that really set tongues a-wagging among K-pop-fixated netizens.

Soon, a few more details of the girl-group project emerged. The group would have five to seven members, still to be selected from YG's pool of trainees; but YG also claimed to be trying something new. Before, they had always looked to pick trainees with talent, but this time good looks were also going to be a major factor in selection: for the first time, they said, they were going to have a super-gorgeous group. Moreover, they insisted that the girls' looks must be natural, putting a clause in their contract that prohibited any plastic surgery.

As proof of their intent, YG officially posted a photo of the first member of this fledgling group. Kim Eunbi looked pretty and pretty cool in her crooked baseball cap, leather jacket and patterned hold-ups. Eunbi had been signed after making the top six of the TV talent show *Superstar K* the previous year. She may not have had plastic surgery, but the accomplished vocalist had certainly lost the cute high-school-student look that she had in the TV series.

Eunbi appeared again in April 2012, this time on a YG-posted YouTube clip alongside another *Superstar K* contestant, Euna Kim. This seventeen-year-old whose charisma had shone through on TV was a New York-born Korean-American, so she fitted the global-facing profile of the new group perfectly. The video, shot in the YG rehearsal room and featuring the two of them singing and rapping their way through Sam Sparro's 'Black and Gold', was an impressive outing for

> Soon, a few more details of the girl-group project emerged. The group would have five to seven members, still to be selected from YG's pool of trainees; but YG also claimed to be trying something new.

trainees. And below-the-line comments show there was plenty of enthusiasm to see more of them.

On 4 May, YG posted a picture on their website of a beautiful young girl sitting cross-legged and looking serious. It was accompanied by just three words: 'Who's that girl?' It didn't take the netizens long to identify her as seventeen-year-old Jennie Kim, a YG trainee supposedly from the Netherlands (although some guessed New Zealand). Another 'Who's that girl?' pic followed two days later. This time it was a black and white photo of a delicate, enigmatic young beauty in a sober jacket and elegant fascinator. She remained a mystery – for now …

This continued on 11 May 2012 with a 'Who's that girl?' video uploaded on YG's YouTube channel. This spotlighted one girl in a group dance to Chris Brown's 'Turn up the Music'. After some impressive moves from the trainee, the video finished on a close-up picture and caption that revealed just her age (sixteen) and the words 'The 5th'. Again, netizens wasted no time in naming her as Lalisa 'Lalice' Manoban from Thailand.

On 29 August 2012, Jennie Kim was the focus of a YG YouTube video featuring a short clip of her covering 'Strange Clouds' by B.o.B. What was particularly interesting was a graphic that appeared in the first few seconds. In an exploding cloud were the words 'Pink Punk'. Did the group now have a name? From what could be gleaned from leaks, news stories and rumours, Pink Punk was the name of YG's new girl group, which some reports now suggested might debut in September 2012. They were said to number seven or even more members. Suddenly they were not being heralded as the new 2NE1, but were being compared to the eight-member Girls' Generation.

September passed, as did a new rumoured debut date in January

2013. Nevertheless, something was definitely happening: 'new YG artist Jennie Kim' played opposite G-Dragon in his video for 'That XX'; an unnamed member with a unique and beguiling accent (later revealed to be Rosé) sang on his track 'Without You' and a YG official revealed that 'all seven members' sang on the chorus of Lee Hi's November 2012 single 'Scarecrow'.

As 2013 began, YG revealed that the answer to 'Who's that girl?' #2 was Kim Jisoo. At that point the word was that Pink Punk was comprised of the four members who would eventually make it to Blackpink, along with Kim Eunbi, Euna Kim and Cho Miyeon (later to debut with (G)I-DLE). Days later, excitement was further generated by a video of Jennie Kim rapping to Wale's 'Lotus Flower Bomb'. However, by June, YG were rethinking the line-up again and an official announcement explained that Euna had left the company for personal reasons (she later confided she had gone due to a lack of confidence in her talents, but she would eventually debut with The Ark) and that, from October, the new group would begin to debut individually in order to gauge the public's reaction.

It didn't happen. Instead fans played spot-the-girls in various YG projects. Lisa was picked out among other YGers dancing in the video to Taeyang's big hit 'Ringa Linga'; there was no missing Jennie when she joined G-Dragon on the TV music show *Inkigayo*, looking divine as she sung her part in his track 'Black'; and Jisoo looked beautiful and won plaudits for her acting in videos for Epik High's 'Spoiler' and 'Happy Ending' and Hi Suhyun's 'I'm Different'.

Meanwhile, Pink Punk rumours rolled on. Unfortunately, Kim Eunbi also had to withdraw from the group, for health reasons, but speculation placed Jang Hanna, a former *Superstar K* contestant, and Jinny Park, another Korean-American, among the possible members of the group. Sometime in 2014, however,

YG abandoned the idea of a nine-member group in favour of a smaller unit. Photos have since emerged of five members – Blackpink plus Cho Miyeon – which many believe to be the group being prepared for a 2015 debut.

Miyeon certainly seemed good-looking and talented enough to be part of the new group and was close to the other girls; her friendships with them continued even after she left YG.

Photos have since emerged of five members – Blackpink plus Cho Miyeon – which many believe to be the group being prepared for a 2015 debut.

Why she didn't debut with them is unclear. Perhaps she got tired of waiting. Maybe YG decided she simply didn't fit. Whatever the reason, she left YG in 2015, emerging three years later when she debuted with (G)I-DLE .

By then there had also been another big step: Pink Punk was no more. Yang Hyun-suk had decided Blackpink sounded much cooler. Jisoo would later recall that other suggested names had included Baby Monster and Magnum, but thankfully these were discarded. By this time, Jennie, Jisoo, Lisa and Rosé were into their fourth or even fifth year of trainee life. On Blackpink's second anniversary they would explain how the delays just made them resolve to work even harder and become even more determined to realize their dream. However, Jennie would also later admit that at times she was scared and began to doubt if she would ever debut.

The friendship these girls had developed was crucial to Yang Hyun-suk's decision to create a four-member group. When they eventually debuted he said that, of all the potential members, they were the closest, and that it was obvious they would make a great team. He even went against K-pop convention and did not name a group leader, saying he believed they could work out any problems or make any decisions among themselves.

Finally, on 18 May 2016, YG confirmed that the line-up had been decided, their debut song had been recorded, the video was being planned and the debut was scheduled for July. Was it finally happening? Two weeks later, as June began, it at last seemed a distinct possibility. YG posted seven pictures under the title 'New Girl Group – Member #1 Jennie'. She was already known from her work with G-Dragon, but these photos revealed Jennie in a number of styles, looking completely gorgeous, whether in a rock T-shirt and tight silver trousers or a demure white shirt, sleeveless jumper and pleated short grey skirt.

True to their promise of revealing a girl each week, next came Lisa, introduced as a five-year trainee from Thailand, who spoke Thai, Korean, English and Japanese. Avid YG watchers had seen her modelling for YG's clothing line, Nonagon, over the last year, but Lisa's pictures showed she could look sultry in a variety of outfits and hair colours, from blonde to auburn to light brown, and excited fans enthused over her beguiling eyes and long legs.

Another familiar face was revealed on 15 June. At the time, Jisoo probably had the highest profile of all the potential members, as she'd modelled in various ads and had even made a cameo appearance in the KBS drama *The Producers*. Her photos also showed a range of concepts and, although the overall impression was of a sweeter, more innocent young woman, one picture, all in white with ripped jeans and her hair tied up, hinted that there was a lot more to come from Jisoo.

Finally, on 22 June came a surprise – at least to those not familiar with every rumour going. 'New Girl Group – Member #4' was

Rosé. YG revealed that she was the mystery singer on G-Dragon's 'Without You', that she was from Australia, nineteen years old, had been a trainee for four years and could play the guitar. Needless to say, she looked pretty wonderful, too. Her features were delicate, her lips full and her hair took on different shades of red or black in the photos as she posed in designer tops, a casual vest and jeans, or a plaid short skirt – but always looking chilled and elegant.

Having unveiled all the members, YG waited another week before divulging the new group's name – Blackpink. It was deliberately chosen, the company explained, to add a twist to the conventional femininity represented by 'pink'. These girls were indeed pretty, but they were also talented and had minds of their own, which was what the 'black' signified. The accompanying photos of all the girls together were amazing; despite all having straight hair past the shoulders and incredible long legs, their looks contrasted and complemented each other to great effect.

This was also when it was announced that YG's Teddy Park, writer and producer for Big Bang and 2NE1, had been working on Blackpink material for some time and had amassed an album's worth of songs already. And, most important of all, in an online poster blazing the legend 'Blackpink In Your Area', their debut was confirmed as 8 p.m. on the eighth day of the eighth month (8 August 2016).

As we moved into July, the excitement continued to grow. Fans now knew who the girls were and

> YG revealed that [Rosé] was the mystery singer on G-Dragon's 'Without You', that she was from Australia, nineteen years old, had been a trainee for five years and could play the guitar.

that Jisoo, born in 1995, was the eldest. Jennie had been born in 1996, and Lisa and Rosé in 1997. Rosé was the tallest, at 168 cm, and Jisoo the shortest, at 162 cm. Jennie was the longest-serving trainee, having clocked up nearly six years, while Rosé, who had been at the company for just over four years, was, relatively speaking, the new girl!

On 3 July, their Instagram account (@blackpinkofficial) was launched with a selection of pictures and a logo – a black circle featuring the word 'BLACKPINK' written across the centre in pink with the A stylized without the cross line and the C and the N both reversed. G-Dragon posted a screenshot of the account to his own Instagram to help them get up and running and within a week, with just five posts, they had amassed over 200,000 followers.

Over the previous five years it had become common for companies debuting major K-pop acts to release pre-debut tracks or music videos. YG had decided against testing the water in this way with Blackpink and were to debut them the old-fashioned way, with some teaser photos and a single-date debut. However, on 6 July, they did upload a dance-practice video of the four girls dancing Parris Goebel and the Royal Family's famous choreography to Rihanna's 'Bitch Better Have My Money'.

Dancing in the company's rehearsal studio, kitted out in various combinations of black crop tops, shorts and leggings, the Blackpink girls were agile and fierce in a video lasting just over a minute. If there were any doubts that the public were primed for Blackpink, this video answered them: it racked up over a million views in just twenty-four hours!

All that remained was for YG to begin the countdown to debut day. From 3 August, each day found new 'Blackpink In Your Area' posters uploaded to their site. The photos ranged from dreamy to cheeky, but once again it was clear that this was not a group that would willingly be categorized. The first day, for instance, saw them looking aloof and cool in T-shirts and matching denim shorts, but an accompanying photo taken from behind saw them each holding a pink pistol behind their backs. The third day had them in a quarry, dressed in white, looking like the last girl gang in town, but on the fourth day they were innocent party girls holding sparklers on a rooftop.

Fans who had waited so long for this ultimate girl group to debut now had an inkling of what lay in store. They knew these girls looked fantastic and had a style of their own – designer wear mixed with street – which they carried off impeccably. They knew they could dance, and all the signs were there that they could sing and rap. And they also knew they were chameleons, able to change from innocent to rebellious in an instant. Yep – it looked like Blackpink were ready to debut.

THREE

DEBUT
WHEN THE HYPE PROVED RIGHT

'I feel like I'm dropping off my daughters on their first day of elementary school,' the *Korea Herald* reported a nervous Yang Hyun-suk saying as his new girl group debuted. 'But I have watched them for the past six years, so I am confident that they will do well. I think the group's performance on stage will speak for itself.'

The K-pop-savvy public already shared his optimism. Their four-year wait had finally come to an end and YG had done its best to bring excitement to boiling point. The video of the group's dance practice had racked up millions of views and the teaser images had been swooned over. Even the titles of their debut twin singles – 'Whistle' and 'Boombayah' – had generated endless discussion online.

The big day was set for 8 August 2016, when an official showcase was scheduled at Moss Studio in Seoul just hours before the release of *Square One*, the mini-album comprising their two debut singles. The showcase took place in front of a small invited audience, but an incredible 450,000 fans logged in to the V Live app to watch as it happened and, after a short video summary of the girls' progress as trainees at YG, they were treated to behind-the-scenes footage from the music videos for the two tracks and the MVs themselves.

The 'making of...' videos showed the four members as fun, sassy and relaxed, but when they finally appeared in person on stage to introduce themselves, they came across as sweet and very nervous. There were cute smiles and glances across at each other, and Jennie managed a quick attempt at *aegyo* (a display of cuteness common among K-pop acts), but they seemed relieved to deliver their message – they promised to work hard and hoped their singles would be well received – and leave.

Still, they looked fantastic – stylish in muted black and grey designer tops and short skirts and shorts. Rosé, with her wavy strawberry-blonde hair, wore a choker, checked blouse and knee-length boots. Jennie, her long hair in a centre parting, had huge sparkling crucifix earrings that matched the embellished collar of her shirt, and short shorts that showed off her long bare legs. Jisoo's long, straight black hair fell over a star-print chiffon dress shaped by a thick belt, while Lisa looked the most edgy of them all, her silver-blonde, green-streaked, shoulder-length hair contrasting with her black padded-shoulder jacket and thigh-high sock boots.

The impact they created made sense of Yang Hyun-suk's words at the press conference that followed. There he explained that YG's customary strategy was to focus on skills and charisma rather than looks, but this time he said the company wanted to put equal emphasis on talent and appearance. He also went to great lengths to account for the long delay in getting his new group to debut. Without naming names, he admitted to rushing some into debuts when they were far from ready. This time, he said, YG were determined to get it right. 'I want to put them on the stage quickly,' he stressed. 'If they go on the stage, there won't be any need for further explanations.'

It was nearly a week until Blackpink were due to make their debut stage performance on TV, so in the meantime fans feasted on the videos, which officially dropped shortly after the showcase. 'Whistle' was certainly

> The girls wasted no time in setting out their 'girl crush' image as they alternated between demure and badass.

eye-catching, as floating camera shots and flashing lights rushed viewers through an array of brightly coloured (with much pink and black), elegant and curious sets, including a red corridor, a blue launderette, a glass-chandelier-lit parking lot and even outer space.

For their part the girls wasted no time in setting out their 'girl crush' image as they alternated between demure and badass. In the video the costumes race by – elegant lace, leather jackets, 1960s-style outfits, baby-doll dresses, sports shorts – while the girls strike some memorable poses. Jisoo appears in a long dress and big boots reading a book in mid-air; Jennie is on horseback – she'd ridden as a child and couldn't wait to shoot this scene; Rosé sits on top of a snow-bound Mini in a pink outfit with glittering powder-blue boots; Lisa in denim on lace bosses it in a big, blue leather armchair; and most iconic of all are the shots of each of them perched on top of the world as if they own it.

As for the song itself, it was laid-back and catchy as anything. Heavy on rhythm and easy on instruments, the whistle is the gimmick, while the refrain of 'Make 'em whistle like a missile' provides an earworm of a hook. Most of all, the song sets out their stall as girls with attitude and showcases all their talents. Jisoo and

Rosé were given restrained but emotional lines, while there was enough meat in Jennie and Lisa's rap parts to show just what they had learned as trainees.

And if that wasn't enough for fans eager to see the new group, 'Boombayah' was released simultaneously. From the unforgettable moment when Jennie drawls 'Blackpink in your area' it was clear it was a classic. To an up-tempo electro-pop backing track zinging with booming bass lines, wailing sirens and a relentless synth hook, the four members deliver a four-minute party anthem brimful of spirit, energy and irresistible charm.

Although there's plenty of pink on display in the MV, this is the black side of Blackpink coming to the fore as the members have fun on mopeds, dance around the house and end up in a jungle. The lyrics don't mess around either. Lisa begins with a rap in English about being a bad girl and wanting a man not a boy, and the others take up the girl-power theme. The message is 'We don't care – we have no fear so don't try to stop us.' They even co-opt the K-pop fans' cry of '*Oppa*' (a Korean word used by women to address older men, sometimes flirtatiously). Jennie later revealed that Yang Hyun-suk had suggested 'Oppa-yah' as the title, but the girls had rejected it, believing it gave the wrong impression of the song.

There's a change of look as the girls parade an edgy rock-chick style with plaid miniskirts, ripped jeans, rock T-shirts, embroidered bomber jackets, chains and chunky boots. Of course, it's all got a sexy side too, with plenty of mesh, chokers, fishnets and garters, and the hair and make-up are still exquisite, from Jennie's neon-pink lipstick to Jisoo's under-eye jewels and from Rosé's sultry pink eyes to Lisa's golden streaks and matching glittering eyeshadow.

And now we really got to see the girls dance. YG had turned to US choreographer Kyle Hanagami, who was already acclaimed for his work for Beyoncé as well as other K-pop acts such as Red Velvet and SNSD (and has since choreographed for BTS, Ariana Grande, Sam Smith and Jennifer Lopez). He produced an incredible routine that stuck to the story: these girls were no shrinking violets. The dance is self-assured, full-on and physical, with arm-swinging, body-rolling and hair flicks galore. But it was fun and cheeky too, especially the rain dance and Rosé's back slide through the members' legs.

> It would take courage and no little self-belief for Blackpink to ignore the haters and let their own talent shine through.

For all the confident posing, there was some trepidation among the group and their company about how they would be received. There was a lot of hype created around them but, unlike most new groups, there had been no pre-debut release to test the waters. Blackpink had to dive headfirst into a crowded and competitive talent pool. Established girl groups such as Wonder Girls, G-Friend and Twice had charting hits, while new groups were emerging all the time with I.O.I, a group from reality TV show *Produce 101*, and the sub-group of Nine Muses both debuting at around the same time.

Then there was the elephant in the room – 2NE1. YG's golden girls were one of the best-selling girl groups of all time and the comparisons were obvious: four good-looking girls, two singers and two rappers, songs from the same writer and producers. For those wanting to disparage YG's new girl group from the outset, 2NE1 were a handy stick to beat them with. It would take courage and no little self-belief for Blackpink to ignore the haters and let their own talent shine through. 'Since they've done a lot of things before us, we want to emulate them,' Lisa said at the showcase, 'but at the same time, we hope there will soon be an opportunity to show our own unique colour.'

On the day after the release of *Square One*, what was clear was that no one was talking about 2NE1. 'Whistle' had gone straight to number one on Korea's eight major real-time, daily and weekly online charts, and would remain at the top for almost a month, with 'Boombayah' simultaneously charting at number two or three. On YouTube it was the reverse, with 'Boombayah' receiving 3 million views in just twenty-one hours and 'Whistle' following closely behind.

By the end of the week, both videos had passed 10 million views, the singles were at the top of the South Korean charts and the world had woken up to Blackpink. *Square One* was topping the iTunes charts in fourteen countries, including Hong Kong, Finland, Colombia and Malaysia, and the two songs were number one and number two on the K-pop weekly chart of China's biggest music-streaming website, QQ Music. What's more, the girls had also taken the top two spots on Billboard's World Digital Songs chart, becoming the first K-pop girl group to hit the top of that chart. They'd picked a good day to go on TV for the first time.

Inkigayo, broadcast on national television at peak time on Sundays, is one of the most prestigious of Korea's many music TV shows. On 14 August it featured both Blackpink singles recorded on the *Inkigayo* stage. If they were nervous this time, the girls certainly didn't show it. 'Whistle' placed them in different 'rooms' of a mocked-up house, before they moved forward to reveal the hypnotizing strutting choreography (devised by, among others, Jonte', who created Beyoncé's 'Single Ladies' dance), while

'Boombayah', strangely performed in front of a huge 3D head, was confidently delivered in all its arm-swinging, hair-flinging glory.

It later emerged that Jennie had sprained her ankle during the dance rehearsal for 'Boombayah' and was taken to hospital for an examination. Despite being in serious pain, she returned to the stage and finished the recording. To her credit, you can't tell she was in any discomfort at all in the broadcast performances. More evidence of the girls' passion came in a video uploaded to Instagram after the recording. It showed Rosé breaking down in tears and other emotional scenes as she and the others were greeted backstage by YG staff. It must have been such an amazing feeling to finally stand together on stage as a group after all those years of hope and hard work.

The girls took to the stage for another stunning performance on *Inkigayo* a week later. Like the other TV music shows, *Inkigayo* presents its own trophy, decided by a combination of chart position, YouTube views and viewer votes. Just thirteen days after debut, Blackpink won that week's *Inkigayo* trophy. It was a monumental achievement and a record for the earliest music-show win for a girl group. Jisoo posted a picture of the girls forming hearts with their hands and wrote, 'Boss, thank you,' for Yang Hyun-suk. He replied, 'It seems the past six years you guys spent training were not in vain. I'm getting emotional too. Congratulations.'

It later emerged that Jennie had sprained her ankle during the dance rehearsal for 'Boombayah' and was taken to hospital for an examination. Despite being in serious pain, she returned to the stage and finished the recording.

For many acts, promoting a single (let alone two!) is a whirlwind of appearances on TV variety and music programmes, radio shows and fan meets. That, however, is not YG's style. The company seemed intent on creating an air of mystery around Blackpink. Despite winning another TV-show trophy (from *M Countdown*) in early September, the group's only appearances were on *Inkigayo* (Jisoo also stood in as MC for the show for one week). And then it was over. YG announced that their performances of 'Whistle' and 'Boombayah' on the 11 September show would end their promotion.

They went out on a high, though. They had exuded more and more charisma with each performance and this final stage was bursting with confidence and personality. It was no surprise to see them take the trophy again, this time bringing Lisa to tears as she was hugged by her bandmates.

In little more than a month Blackpink had shown the world what they were about. They could sing and rap, they could act girly or savage, they could dance with swagger and sensuality, and they looked fabulous – always. In just a few performances the members had established their own style as a group and as individuals. It was reported that within a couple of weeks of their debut they had already received more than ten offers to model in TV ads. Blackpink were definitely going places and fans were already signed up for the journey.

FOUR

COMEBACK

No sooner had they arrived than they disappeared again. For a little over a month, Blackpink had been the talk of K-pop, dominating the charts and the online forums. Their handful of appearances had established that they looked stylish and fabulous and were capable of pulling off complex choreography, too. Their debut might have been short, but it was incredibly sweet.

At the end of September, YG officials admitted that even they had been taken by surprise by the success of the group. They also acknowledged fans' pleas for the group to appear on TV variety shows or in their own reality series. They re-stated their plans to promote the group through musical performances, but 'in order to repay fans' support' agreed to consider such appearances.

After waiting such a long time to debut, the girls were naturally on a high. There was always going to be some sniping, and some haters kept up the 'not as good as 2NE1' jibes, but the public reaction to the two singles had been amazing. Blackpink were even making waves in the USA, with *Rolling Stone* magazine including them in their '10 New Artists You Need to Know' list (along with Dua Lipa) and *Entertainment Weekly* noting that Blackpink wouldn't be entirely out of place in the US charts as they placed them among their 'Emerging Artists You Need to Hear Now'.

Another measure of their success came as a Korean research company revealed they were the girl group with the highest brand reputation. It was the first time a new group had gone straight to the top of the rankings. This was borne out when they were appointed brand ambassadors for Reebok Classics, resulting in a feature in the fashion and streetwear publication *1st Look* – their first magazine spread. In a campervan road-trip-themed photo shoot, the girls proved they could dress down and still look stunning with their long, bare legs bringing full attention to the trainers.

At the same time YG's cosmetics company, Moonshot, had some products of their own to promote, and who better to employ than their own super-brand princesses? Blackpink's members became the official models for the launch of a new lipstick collection called Lip Feat. Each of the girls promoted four different shades: sweet Jisoo in plaits showed off a bold lippy from her Electronic Pink options; Jennie's vibrant mauve lipstick was from her Hip Hop Purple range; Lisa winked as she pouted her luscious Modern Rock Red lips; and Rosé went subtle, an orangey-pink from her Acoustic Nude selection perfectly matching her light-red hair.

The girls explained how, through spending all their working, sleeping and leisure time together, they had become such great friends.

In October they made the cover of popular culture magazine *Nylon*. They looked intense (even slightly scary!) staring out from the front page. But they were also sublime in delicate white or pale-cream cotton tops, with only Rosé's big boots and Lisa's frayed denim shorts hinting at another side to the girls. Inside the magazine the girls displayed their modelling prowess, even taking some fashion risks as Jisoo wore a corset outside her jacket and Jennie (now sporting ombré hair) posed in a grey herringbone coat with brown suede arms and fur cuffs.

The *Nylon* interview gave us a chance to discover a little more about these performers who had been kept under such tight wraps. The girls explained how, through spending all their working, sleeping and leisure time together, they had become such great friends. Jennie expressed how she loves the charm in Rosé's singing voice, something she said you don't find in Korea; Lisa told how Jisoo is the mood-maker, continuously telling jokes and making them laugh; Jennie was named the group's fashionista on account of her ever-surprising wardrobe; and Lisa, so Rosé informed us, is so beautiful, inside and out.

Although a month had passed, they were still taking in the excitement of finally debuting. They were naturally pleased with how it had gone, but Jisoo was critical of her dancing ability and Lisa said she needed to work on her Korean pronunciation. They also revealed how they liked to spend their spare time, with Jennie saying she enjoyed taking pictures with her old-fashioned film camera, and Rosé admitting she had missed playing the piano and guitar during the debut, saying her hands became stiff if she didn't play regularly. The article finished with the girls confirming that a new song was coming soon – one in which they hoped even more of their talents would be revealed.

The growing legions of Blackpink fans didn't have long to wait. On 19 October YG posted a new 'Who's Next?' teaser. This time it was Blackpink themselves who were next. The following day it was revealed that Blackpink's comeback was happening on the first day of November. In K-pop any new release is termed a 'comeback' and it may (but doesn't have to) involve a new look, concept or sound. The first comeback is particularly crucial as its success can determine if an act is a one-hit wonder or is here to stay.

The week before the stated release date saw YG repeat the countdown formula. Gradually it transpired that another two new tracks – 'Playing with Fire' and 'Stay' – would be released simultaneously (with the digital release also featuring an acoustic version of 'Whistle'), while the teaser pics and video clips shared the ethereal look and soft yellow filter of the *Nylon* shoot.

Releasing 'making of...' videos as teasers was unusual, but it was a trick YG had employed with other groups, so it wasn't a complete surprise to find that the final two teasers featured 'behind the scenes' videos of each of the new tracks. At last fans really felt they were getting to know the group members. There was little doubt they were close friends, caring for one other and completely at ease in each other's company. In special moments – including the sheet of paper caught in the wind that lands neatly on Jisoo's head, Lisa getting spooked out in the derelict house, Rosé being teased when she hugs the boy, and the Jennie-cam interview with Jisoo – their characters shone through. They were also completely charming, cute, fun and, of course, naturally gorgeous.

When the actual tracks dropped, the first reaction was that they lacked the gimmicky, out-there quality of the debut tracks. Soon, however, they were being acknowledged as very different but well-crafted pop songs that enabled the girls to show their versatility and their vocal skills. 'Playing with Fire' was built around an on-trend tropical-synth sound, but it was very much a pop song and a distinct Blackpink pop song at that. It's full of catchy and completely addictive components, from the plinky-plonky piano to the bass hook and the bubbling electronic sound, but most of all it's the vocals that grab the listener.

In an interview with *Ten Asia*, Jennie had explained that the song compares the excitement and danger of being in love to playing with fire. However, the group confessed to never having experienced those kinds of emotions themselves, admitting that their understanding of romance mainly came from watching movies and TV dramas together in the dorm. 'When a romantic scene comes on,' said Jisoo, 'we hold on to each other and scream.' Not that you would sense any unfamiliarity from their vocal performances. The delivery is the standout aspect of the song. Each of them has a distinct part, but the four voices blend seamlessly. Even to those who struggle to understand the language, the rhymes, rhythm and flow of the lyrics and cheeky English lines all give the song a unique charm and appeal.

The simultaneous release, 'Stay', followed this pattern of giving each member their own part, but it was a totally different sound. 'Stay' had a timeless folky feel with just a soft acoustic guitar and hand-clap backing to a softly sung plea for a lover not to leave. Again, YG played with the format, taking a singer-songwriter style of track but adding a rap part – Lisa's downbeat spoken rap dovetails perfectly with the vocals – and the now expected earworm hook of the 'Lalala-lalala' chorus.

If the intention of each of the new tracks was to show off the girls' vocal talents, then the videos seemed focused on showing us just how good they each looked. 'Playing with Fire' combined a choreography set with slo-mo clips of the members looking sultry and moody. Assuming the aim was to reinforce their stylish image, it worked perfectly. They performed the choreography in killer outfits. Jisoo wore a patchwork satin dress with red patches that matched her now strawberry hair, Rosé was in space-age silver, Lisa was in a fabulous neck-tie fil-coupé blouse with multicoloured squares and gold chevron sleeves, and Jennie wore a floral crêpe top. Though variously colourful and shiny, the look was given coherence by the big ring-buckle black belts they all wore.

The video for 'Stay' was more about creating an atmosphere, with the subdued colours and post-apocalyptic (or perhaps post-party!) scenes emphasizing the tone of the song. Of course, though, the members all looked great still and there were some iconic visuals, including Jisoo on the swing in her long yellow dress, Lisa dancing alone in the corridor in her stunning red mohair jacket (with appliqué horses' heads) and the four of them standing on an upturned vehicle looking out at the city as four fireworks coloured the air.

Though neither song reached the heights of the previous releases in the South Korean charts (although both made the top ten), it was clear the group was establishing a fan base at home and internationally. In just twenty-four hours 'Playing with Fire' hit around 4.3 million views while 'Stay' passed the 3.5 million mark. 'Playing with Fire' earned them a second number one on the Billboard World Digital Songs chart, while 'Stay' reached number four. They had also begun to make an impact on other

Billboard charts, as well as breaching the Top 100 in Japan and, more surprisingly, Canada.

Blackpink had their comeback stage on *Inkigayo* on 6 November 2016. They performed 'Stay' first and it was completely magical. In an autumn-themed set with starry skies and red and golden trees, they each sat on leafy vine-covered swings, taking to the floor only for the final part of the song. Each of the members was appropriately dressed in warm clothes: Lisa in a short fur-trimmed black dress dotted with large pearls, Rosé in a white shirt with embroidered bodice, Jennie in a striking pink and turquoise hooped sweater and Jisoo in a blue chambray shirt with a delicate lace collar. Their vocals were spot-on, with the quality of Jennie and Rosé's voices receiving particular attention when the video appeared on YouTube.

In contrast, the 'Playing with Fire' performance took place on a dance floor surrounded by neon comic-horror motifs and was all about the choreography; the swag, the energy, the endless expressive hand movements and the flicks of their perfect long hair all contributing to a dance packed full of surprise and delight. And if Jisoo was still lacking confidence in her dancing, it was clear she had come on in leaps and bounds in the few months since their debut. This was all aided by YG, which had splashed out on custom-made head microphones. Previously they had used hand mics, which had inhibited the choreography, or mics taped to their cheeks, which could irritate their skin and move around, but these new white headset-style mics were stylish and allowed them to dance with complete freedom.

The fact that the group hadn't mimed, but had sung both tracks live (although 'Stay' was pre-recorded), had not been missed by K-pop fans. YG clearly had complete confidence in the girls' vocal abilities and they rose to the occasion, even while performing the dance routine. K-pop has developed its own slang and one phrase was especially prevalent after this performance: CD-eating. No one was really suggesting that YG were grinding CDs into powder to feed to their artists to make them sound perfect, but saying they'd had CDs for breakfast was a fun way of saying that the Blackpink members had a magical ability to sing just as well on stage as they did in the recording studio.

Fans had one more moment of excitement in store. As the winners' announcement took place, Jennie and Jisoo were seen hugging and congratulating Nayeon of trophy-winning group Twice. The clear friendship between the three was important as many were building up the two rookie girl groups as fierce rivals, a situation that always has the potential to get out of hand and become toxic as fans take sides on various internet forums.

It was a well-known fact that YG artists rarely performed on any music shows other than *Inkigayo*. Yang Hyun-suk was on record as saying he felt it was the only show that presented his artists – through the camerawork and sets – as he would like. Mind you, certain exceptions were occasionally made, and this was the case with Blackpink's comeback. Just four days after their *Inkigayo* appearance, they performed on *M Countdown*. The 'Playing with Fire' set, all shabby chic and neon with bursts of flames, couldn't have displeased Yang Hyun-suk and, once again singing live, the girls – in their outfits from the MV – smashed it.

M Countdown's 'Stay' set had none of the *Inkigayo* autumn theme, but muted lights and orange spotlights with the girls on stools rather than swings. However, the group's own style was pure Blackpink: super sophisticated, but with their own twists of colour. Jisoo (her hair now a deep chestnut) wore a high-collared shiny pink dress, Jennie was in a patterned skirt suit, Rosé matched a fringed top with a tiered red mini and Lisa had a high-contrast red and blue blouse.

Blackpink returned to *Inkigayo* to perform 'Playing with Fire' on every show for the next five weeks and the track continued to fly high in the charts. The intricacies of how *Inkigayo* calculated its competition (Blackpink were not able to earn album points) meant the group were narrowly pipped to the Best Single award by Twice for three weeks running. However, by the end of November, Blackpink finally took the award, beating established acts SHINee and Taeyeon. Fittingly, Twice (who, having won three times running, were exempt) were there to pay back the affection they had received, warmly congratulating the girls at the show's finale.

The following week Blackpink would win again, but now the promotion was drawing to a close. They held their *Inkigayo* goodbye stage on 11 December and again looked sensational, managing to mix classy dresses and designer wear with PVC skirts and knee-high sports socks, always with small elements – belts, colours or styles – linking the group. In their short interview, they promised to be back sooner and to work even harder to improve.

Despite their promotions being once again limited, the comeback had been successful. They had won over many new fans, developed a style of their own and demonstrated that they were more than just pretty faces. They had chart success and had

Blackpink returned to *Inkigayo* to perform 'Playing with Fire' on every show for the next five weeks and the track continued to fly high in the charts.

notched up music-show awards; pretty good going for a rookie group. The next big test would come very soon as the awards season began to get under way. Had they shown enough to be recognized as a new force in K-pop?

FIVE

ROOKIE QUEENS

As the promotions for 'Playing with Fire' and 'Stay' came to an end, Blackpink were able to look back at a pretty successful six months since their debut. All their singles had been well received and had charted well in South Korea, and they had been particularly successful in establishing a core of international fans. K-pop fans in Japan, China and South-East Asia were quick to support the group, but Blackpink also had fan bases as far afield as Europe and North America. By the year's end, this international following had helped Blackpink's first two releases rank among YouTube's most watched K-pop videos of 2016, with 'Boombayah' placed sixth on 80 million views and 'Whistle' placed eighth on 65 million.

The members had now established themselves as talented singers, rappers and dancers, and no one was in any doubt as to their beauty. It was especially noticeable that fans had not focused on one or even two members, but rather each of the girls had garnered considerable attention. This is clear from the online forums and below-the-line comments on Blackpink videos, where fans talk about their favourites or, in K-pop terminology, their 'bias'. Many fans would admit their bias had changed after a

> Most groups in their first year, when they are known as 'rookie groups', court publicity, appearing on as many TV shows as they can; if possible, they may even have their own dedicated reality or variety show.

particular performance or would refer to a member as a 'bias-wrecker' after they had performed so well or looked so good that they now threatened the top spot of their favourite.

The only problem with Blackpink was that there had been so little exposure of each of the girls; it was difficult for fans to feel they really knew any of them. Most groups in their first year, when they are known as 'rookie groups', court publicity, appearing on as many TV shows as they can; if possible, they may even have their own dedicated reality or variety show. Blackpink had performed on music shows, but aside from very brief interviews and behind-the-scenes videos, they had been women of mystery. However, in December 2016, that was all about to change …

The live streaming app V Live was launched in 2015 and immediately opened K-pop up to international fans. This app allows K-pop groups to not only upload recorded videos, but also to post live from their dorms, studio or hotel rooms, or even from dressing rooms prior to concerts. Most excitingly, the app enables fans to message their idols while they are posting and, if they are lucky, to hear a live reply. Fans around the world are encouraged to participate, with subtitles usually appearing within hours of the transmission.

After their appearance on *M Countdown* was broadcast on 10 November, Blackpink posted their first V Live chat. It's just a five-minute broadcast from their car where they say hello and introduce themselves (though of course most fans knew who they were already!). They were new to the concept and they struggled to say anything meaningful – at one point they even had to make it clear that the screen hadn't frozen; it was just that they weren't saying anything! – but it was a start.

A few days later, they were posting again, this time from the sofa in their dorm. Here they all appeared to be holding dolls or toy animals: Jennie had the alien from *Toy Story*, Rosé had a cute duck and Lisa held a pink-booted unicorn (next to Jennie's T-shirt, which read 'unicorns are real'). Soon fans realized that Jisoo wasn't holding a fluffy toy but instead had a real dog on her lap – a super-cute white Maltese puppy whom she introduced as Dalgom. The girls were much more relaxed in their own home. They spoke Thai, Japanese, Spanish and English as well as Korean and appeared with minimal make-up, but of course they still looked amazing.

One more fact emerged from this broadcast, although it was no secret to avid fans: Blackpink were to appear on the TV show *Weekly Idol*. Hosted by comedian Jeong Hyeong-don and rapper Defconn, *Weekly Idol* is one of the longest-running and most popular of Korea's many variety shows. Over sixty minutes, guests, often from the same group, chat, perform and undergo fun challenges. It is a chance for fans to see their idols' charisma and charm, so appearing on the show is a great opportunity for any new group.

Blackpink's *Weekly Idol* episode was broadcast on 16 November and it was a triumph. The girls were initially shy and nervous, but the hosts are masters at putting their guests at ease. From the moment Rosé joked that Jeong Hyeong-don looked just like her father, the members were relaxed and so much fun. Jisoo, the eldest of the girls, was the most animated, admitting to having a 4D personality (a K-pop term for an idol who is wacky and extra), while Lisa reminded everyone she was the *maknae* (the youngest) of the group and that the others took care of her. Jennie said hello to her puppies Kai and Kuma ('And Dalgom,' shouted Jisoo), and did a hilarious impression of their boss.

Then they faced the random-play dance, a favourite segment of the show. Here the group had to perform the correct choreography to randomly selected clips of their tracks. Fortunately, Blackpink had only four songs to choose from, so they handled it pretty well – until Jennie barged Jisoo out of her way and had to accept the punishment, a strike with a soft hammer from Defconn. She was very funny, claiming she had a 'low pain tolerance' and then collapsing into fits of giggles after being hit.

Next up was the section of the show where the hosts looked at the member's self-written profiles, teasing and testing each of them. Jisoo proceeded to prove that she can play the *buk* (a traditional Korean drum) and then she explained her nicknames for the others. Jendeukie (for Jennie) was the sweetest and Pasta (for Rosé) the strangest (after the dish rosé pasta), while Lisa's were plays on the Korean words *Kokkili-sa*, meaning elephant, or *Jolisa*, meaning chef, for when she was cooking. Jisoo even gave herself a nickname, Chichu. As Hyeong-don pointed out, she had kept the cutest name for herself!

Jisoo was cute, chatty and very funny, and the others took her lead. Jennie got them singing the song with which they greet their YG boss (then admitting he just ignores them and walks past), Rosé played the guitar and sang a bewitching cover of B.o.B's 'Not for Long' and, along with Jisoo, made a fine attempt at performing the dances to K-pop classics 'Good Boy' and 'Ringa Linga'. Lisa, perhaps not so confident in her Korean, said the least, but still managed to surprise with some well-executed B-Girl moves. Finally, the four took on the double-speed dance challenge, perfectly running through a speeded-up 'Boombayah'.

Their appearance on the show must have given them such confidence. Jisoo and Rosé were real stars, the former for her zany personality and sense of humour and the latter for her captivating speaking and singing voice, but the other two had also played their parts in showing Blackpink to be a group full of charisma and surprises. This was reinforced a few weeks later when they appeared on celebrity game show *Running Man*. As they joined in the fun games, with Lisa and Jisoo on Team Black and Rosé and Jennie on Team Pink, we discovered that they all have a great sense of humour and are up for anything – and that Jennie is extremely competitive!

It wasn't clear whether YG had changed its mind or it was always the plan, but the Blackpink cat was now out of the bag. There were magazine interviews and more V Live posts, including a Lie-V, a soothing late Sunday evening 'lie-down show' that featured the girls relaxing on cushions and blankets as if they were having a sleepover, reading fans' comments and telling stories. They talked about how they felt strange hearing their songs in

> Jisoo and Rosé were real stars, the former for her zany personality and sense of humour and the latter for her captivating speaking and singing voice, but the other two had also played their parts in showing Blackpink to be a group full of charisma and surprises.

public and how they were still shocked at being recognized when they were out and about. They shared memories of when they first met and of trainee days, including one amusing story of how, after they were exhausted from endless training, they spelt out 'SOS' with their bodies, knowing the head of the company sometimes watched them practise on a camera. The next day they were given a surprise day off! As the fifty-minute conversation moved from subject to subject, we realized just how close these girls were and that they had more or less selected themselves to become a group.

Whether the public and critics approved of that selection was about to become evident. Winter in K-pop is awards season and awards are mega-important. They involve star-packed shows, with celebrities both on stage and in the audience, and the prizes are keenly studied by K-pop fans. As YG's latest protégées there was a great deal of pressure on Blackpink to pick up some of the awards up for grabs for new acts. 'Honestly, it would be a lie if we said we weren't hoping for a rookie award,' they told *Star News*. 'If we were to really win one, it would be amazing.'

Although all awards are gratefully received, in K-pop some have more significance than others. Melon Music Awards (MMA) and Mnet Asian Music Awards (MAMA), both pre-Christmas events, are among the most coveted prizes. To receive a rookie award at either of these would have been on Blackpink's list of ambitions when they debuted. The MMAs in November came up first and Blackpink were not only attending but also performing at the all-star show.

The MMAs at the Gocheok Sky Dome baseball stadium in Seoul saw Blackpink appear on stage in their biggest live performance yet. If they were nervous no one would have guessed, as the performances were completely awesome. First they sang 'Whistle', looking like four snow queens in front of an incredible ice-palace setting. They were all dressed in white but, as we were by now accustomed to seeing, their outfits were not identical. Lisa's dress was simple, tight and embellished; Rosé's lace top and pleated skirt radiated pure style; Jennie looked so cute wrapped in a fur jacket; and Jisoo's outfit was delicate and feminine.

Later, when they came strutting out to perform 'Playing with Fire' in chic red and black outfits, their versatility took many viewers' breath away. They could carry off totally different vibes, look great and perform the kind of complex and energetic choreography that up to now had generally been the province of boy bands. They were still in the red and black when they were called up to collect the award for Best New Artist. Rosé stepped forward to give the acceptance speech, instantly winning over loads of new fans, who immediately fell for her cute shyness and Aussie-tinged Korean accent. A few days later it was Jennie's turn to speak as they picked up their second rookie award at the first-ever Asia Artist Awards.

An unavoidable truth about awards shows is that they are sometimes controversial. This came into focus at the MAMAs in early December. For a number of reasons, YG did not send its major names to the high-profile awards show in Hong Kong, and many believed this led to Blackpink losing out to I.O.I for the prestigious Best New Artist award. They couldn't ignore the girls completely, though, as they picked up a consolation prize, the Best of Next Female Artist award.

Blackpink celebrated their first Christmas together with a performance at the most celebrated of all the season's TV music festivals, *SBS Gayo Daejun*. It was another blistering performance and the post-show internet forums reverberated with two topics. One was Jennie's red-hot twerking, with many claiming this was the show that really brought her to the fore. The other was the love-in between the girls and boy band BTS, who were now achieving massive success at home and internationally, having broken through in the USA. Vocalist Jungkook, who had already admitted to being a Blackpink fan, led his bandmates as they danced along to 'Whistle' and 'Playing with Fire', while the girls happily bopped away when the Bangtan boys took to the stage.

The festival featured Blackpink members in other units as well. Jennie performed with a street-dance team that also included SHINee's Taemin, GOT7's Jinyoung and Yugyeom, NCT's Ten, Red Velvet's Seulgi, Oh My Girl's YooA and DIA's Eunjin. Then Rosé featured in a special 'acoustic stage'. Backed by indie duo 10cm, EXO's Chanyeol and Twice's Jihyo, she played guitar and sang a beautiful acoustic version of 'Whistle'.

So 2016 was coming to an end and what a year it had been for the members of Blackpink. They took stock as they wished their fans a happy New Year on Twitter, picking out their highlights of the last twelve months. Their debut broadcast on *Inkigayo* when they got to meet their fans for the first time, their first-ever music-show win and their first rookie award were clearly moments that they would savour forever.

And what did 2017 hold in store? Fans' New Year hopes centred on hearing new tracks from Blackpink, with rumours that YG were preparing a mini-album. They also looked forward to the group collecting more awards in the forthcoming and highly prestigious shows and, after the variety-show successes, they were hopeful they would have a chance to see the members in their own series. Finally, they desperately wished for YG to recognize the fans with an official fan club and a fan name they could be all be proud of. These were indeed exciting times ...

SIX

AS IF…

One of the major characteristics that differentiate K-pop acts from their Western counterparts is the fan base. K-pop fans are passionate, vocal and supportive and consume not just the music but any photograph, message or snippet of news about their idols, too. In a word, obsessive – but not in a bad way. Without their votes, online views, sharing of information and, of course, purchase of tracks, an act has little chance of success. So every act loves and cultivates its fandom, sending messages, appearing at fan meetings and making V Live broadcasts, hoping their fans can reach the levels of BTS's ARMY or EXO's EXO-L.

The fandom name is important. It gives fans a sense of identity and ties them inextricably to their idols. Apart from ARMY and EXO-L, the most famous include Girls' Generation's SONE ('So One'), Big Bang's VIPs, GOT7's iGOT7 (aka ahgase) and Red Velvet's ReVeluv. The best names are witty and relate to the group. 2NE1's Blackjack (21 in playing cards) and Twice's Once are great examples. Most groups name their fandoms by the end of their debut year. Blackpink's rivals from JYP, Twice, had announced their fan name in November 2015, although Red Velvet, who had debuted in 2014, took until April 2017 to name theirs.

Through their various stage and online interactions, it had become clear that Blackpink had already established a large and devoted following. Many of them were wondering when YG would announce a fandom name and were busy coming up with their own suggestions, such as Pink Mafia or PinkBlack. Then, on 14 January, enigmatic as ever, an image appeared on the official Blackpink Instagram account that featured only one word: Blink. Of course, fans went into overdrive as they tried to guess what it meant. Was it a comeback announcement or a fandom name?

Two days later, on the same account, Jennie posted a thank-you to fans for her birthday wishes and presents and, in doing so, confirmed the fans' name. 'BLINK my favorite people on this planet,' she wrote. 'I can't thank you guys enough for all the gifts and letters.' And she finished the message with, 'I love you my blinks.' Fans were ecstatic. The portmanteau word, made up of black and pink, was clever, cute and cool – just like the group themselves.

That wasn't the only excitement for the new Blinks. The Golden Disc Awards were taking place at the very same time. Dubbed the 'Korean Grammys', the ceremony is arguably Korea's most prestigious music-awards event and Blackpink were a star attraction on only their first visit. From the second they stepped on to the red carpet to their performances of 'Playing with Fire' and

'Whistle', to the seemingly inevitable moment when they collected the Best New Artist Award, they got the cameras flashing.

Their stylists had been bold with sparkling black and contrast-coloured outfits that were individual and yet presented a unified style, whether through buttoned-up collars, glittering belts or skirts, dresses and shorts all cut to the same length. Jisoo's plain black pinafore dress contrasted with her shimmering silver chiffon blouse and bejewelled belt; Lisa stood out in a pink Marc Jacobs shirt covered in small metallic dots with a black pussy bow fastened with a silver brooch; and Jennie was chic and pretty in a silk Saint Laurent music-note-print minidress with customized sequinned cuffs and collar, set off with silver belt and choker. This time, though, it was Rosé who was possibly the most eye-catching, which isn't easy in that line-up. Now with her hair a very light strawberry blonde, she looked so elegant in a shiny and fluffy peach shirt and black wrap miniskirt with military brocade. It was the brocade on the skirt, the rows of pearls and the large glittering crucifix that took her cool levels off the scale.

A week later it was a similar story at the Seoul Music Awards, the final prestigious ceremony of the season. They rocked the red carpet in black and silver, especially Jennie in a Victorian-style ruffle dress and Jisoo in an embellished A-line silk minidress, and then hit the stage with Rosé in a fabulous red, yellow and blue chevron knit dress. They got EXO and BTS bouncing, mouthing the words and copying their dance moves in their seats, and proceeded to pick up the Best New Artist Award again.

Incredibly, Blackpink had achieved all this on just four songs and with very little exposure to the public. Since February, Jisoo had been the regular MC on *Inkigayo* (a role she would continue for a whole year) and was proving a popular choice, but the others were relatively unknown. The one thing K-pop fans did associate them with, however, was style and beauty. This was clear in February 2017, when they appeared on the variety show whose title translates as *Get it Beauty*.

In the show they shared their beauty tips and revealed their favourite cosmetics items. Jisoo said she had dry skin and focused on skincare, using face masks two or three times a day, Rosé said she tended to stick to tried-and-tested shades that she knew complemented her looks, and Jennie revealed her love of limited-edition products, but it was Lisa who emerged as the most obsessed with cosmetics. Rosé joked that her friend would go out shopping all day for products and then come home and continue shopping online, while the hosts dubbed her Cosmetics Mansour – a reference to the wealthy United Arab Emirates politician and royal Sheikh Mansour.

For all their success, Blackpink were yet to play their own concert, but as the spring months arrived they were at last ready to meet their public. The moment finally came during YG's UNICEF Walking Festival, a charity event featuring many of the YG Family. This was followed by other short performances – still from their limited repertoire – at the annual Korean University festivals.

Talk was now strong of an imminent Blackpink comeback. On 5 June, a YG official revealed that a music video was being filmed that week and on 13 June a single picture of ornate pillars and a frieze on the official website bore the confirmation of a 22 June comeback. Then came the drip-feed of the teaser photos. Jennie was first, looking innocent in a plain red top, her hair in twin ponytails with matching red scrunchies. Only the beads covering her forearm betrayed any sophistication. Similarly, her make-up was minimalist: pale lips and a little brown shadow on the outside of intense staring eyes.

Next was Jisoo in a heart-print fringed shirt paired with large gold rings and dangling earrings. She, too, had an innocent aura, accented by similar simple make-up and two thin hair braids. Rosé had more of a playful schoolgirl style with pink lips, a pink Gucci Modern Future hoodie, pink fishnets and denim shorts with a white belt. But what was really stunning was her hair: parted off-centre with one thick braid, it was dark! We'd only seen her in reddish blonde or orange until now.

One fan asked which member they would date if they were a guy. Lisa jokingly chose herself.

Finally came Lisa, who, it seemed, hadn't received the innocent memo. She was more of a temptress in a blue striped towelling crop top, frayed denim shorts and thigh-high pale-pink boots. With her now long orange hair (and self-cut bangs), thick silver upper-arm bracelet and 'don't mess with me' stare, she was definitely channelling the black side of Blackpink!

It was now apparent that Blinks, who had been hoping for an album, would have to make do with just one track. On release day – 22 June 2017 – the girls introduced the new single, 'As If It's Your Last', in a V Live broadcast from their Blackpink pop-up store in Seoul. A confident Jisoo, clearly benefitting from her *Inkigayo* MCing (the others call her 'MC Chu'), took control, but this was super-fun Blackpink, all having a laugh with and at each other. It was full of lovely moments, such as Jennie saying she wanted to drive an ice-cream van, Jisoo piping up with her made-up meaningless word 'ppoong' and Lisa making up a song about how great her mum was. One fan asked which member they would date if they were a guy. Lisa jokingly chose herself before picking Jennie ('because she's hot'); Jisoo picked Rosé, as she'd write and sing songs for her on the guitar; and Rosé chose Jennie for her kimchi fried rice.

As YG and the group themselves said, the new track – with lyrics describing an all-consuming love – was a contrast to their previous tracks. According to the group this was the 'pink' side of Blackpink emerging: positive with plenty of zip and energy. They described it as the perfect summer song, recalling how they couldn't help but dance and sing along when they first heard it. Some classified it as 'moombahton' – a combination of house music and reggaeton – and although the bass, drums and synth drive the song along, the chorus is pure pop, belted out by Jennie and Rosé. It is still in a distinctive Blackpink style, with the girls' vocals playing off each other, the catchy stuttered line of 'ma-ma-majimakcheoreom' and Lisa rapping her whole part in English. There's also a nice touch in the reprise of their line 'Blackpink in your area'. All in all it was the perfect summer bop.

The music video for 'As If It's Your Last' echoed the upbeat theme. It had no plot to speak of, but looked fabulous. Quickfire editing produced an array of settings from the spectacular pink columns to a subway station, a yellow parking lot, a bedroom full of cuddly toys, an elegant lounge, a kaleidoscopic tunnel, a vintage American convertible car and Jennie's ice-cream truck. It is a feast of neon and pastel, especially pink. The sunshine factor is reflected in the girls' moods, too. Although the 'black' side is still there in the occasional teasing or daring looks and glances, smiles and contentment are the order of the day, with a great sense of camaraderie on display when the four are together.

Pink is also ever-present among the maelstrom of costumes that appear as the video cuts from location to location. The central pillars scene finds them in black and white schoolgirl

ABOVE At their first major award show, the 2016 Melon Music Awards, Blackpink showed that a girl group can have individual styles.

ABOVE Showing off their charm and talent in Japan, 2017.

BELOW Incredibly cute and impeccably stylish. Blackpink on their way to pick up the Greatest Girl Group trophy at the SBS Awards in 2017.

These girls had been best friends for over six years by 2018. No wonder they feel so at ease with each other.

With iconic
outfits and
fabulous performances,
Blackpink had a whole lot of
fun at Coachella in April 2019.

ABOVE Black and white, dark and blonde, Blackpink rock the 2019 Gaon Chart Awards show.

BELOW Designer brands to the fore, the girls look incredible as they are introduced to the US at the LA Artist Showcase in February 2019.

ABOVE The very definition of 'airport style'. Jisoo and Jennie at Incheon Airport in 2019.

LEFT Sophisticated and beautiful. Lisa and Rosé attend the Mulberry A/W event in Seoul in 2018.

OVERLEAF Blackpink are amazed by the number of fans greeting them in Times Square for their 2019 *Good Morning America* appearance.

outfits (which enabled Lisa to get excited about wearing Korean school uniform, although it's doubtful whether garter phone holsters were regulation anywhere!). However, bolder colours immediately break out in abundance. Ties, earrings, hair slides and bracelets keep the pink theme going, while allowing the girls to keep the colour factor at peak with any number of high-fashion garments, from Rosé's zingy heart-print minidress to Jennie's Indian-style floral crop top and brocade skirt, or from Jisoo's amazing flaming-blue platform shoes to Lisa's multicoloured Anna Sui New York bomber jacket. The list, a bottomless-budget stylist's dream, goes on and on.

Once again, a dance-practice video was posted on YouTube just two days after the release date and back in the YG studio the girls, through their clothes and their choreography, still manage to convey a sense of both togetherness and individuality. They are all basically dressed in black, but each of the members is distinctive: Jennie with long trousers, Jisoo wearing an oversized T-shirt, Lisa sporting a red and white striped cap and Rosé in a white crop top. Similarly, they all have individual roles in the dance, but come together, even linking arms, to dance as one unit. This choreography continued to establish a Blackpink style of high-energy complex movements, hair flicks, finger points and gimmicks, such as Rosé sliding through the others' legs (again). However, knowing Blinks would attempt the dance, they also deliberately included some simpler moves.

The full choreography was also on display when they appeared on the weekly music shows. The girls wore their school uniforms (starting something of a fashion trend) in their first comeback stage on *Show! Music Core* and then dressed in various colourful outfits from the video as they appeared on that show and *Inkigayo* every week for the next month. On the latter show, Blackpink took three consecutive trophies (known as a triple crown) and at the same time they were also breaking records for the most viewed K-pop music video, with over 13 million views in twenty-four hours and 75 million over the four weeks after release. It became their third single to debut at number one on Billboard's World Digital Song Sales chart and their first song to crack the Billboard Bubbling Under Hot 100 chart, where it reached number thirteen (this was in their first year – BTS took four years to achieve the same feat!). Meanwhile, the track reached number one on the iTunes Worldwide Singles charts in twenty-five countries and charted in another seventy-five countries.

> On [Inkigayo] Blackpink took three consecutive trophies (known as a triple crown) and at the same time they were also breaking records for the most viewed K-pop music video, with over 13 million views in twenty-four hours.

True to their word, YG were allowing Blackpink more exposure throughout the promotion period. They returned for more fun on *Weekly Idol*, where they demonstrated the original ending to the choreography with them spelling out L-O-V-E with their fingers. They also made their debut on the popular variety show *Knowing Bros*, where their school uniforms were a perfect fit for the classroom setting (and Jisoo showed off her purple hair). Now much more at ease, they were a massive hit, displaying their innocent, fun and mischievous sides.

Indeed, in the height of summer 2017 in South Korea it was difficult to miss Blackpink. They appeared looking gorgeous in black or white dresses in the style magazine *High Cut*, and they were glamorous cover stars for *Elle Korea*. In a photoshoot that graced several pages they posed in clothing from the luxury brand Saint Laurent, designed by Anthony Vaccarello, looking completely chic and classy. Some fans even got to meet the girls in person when they hosted fan meetings, including a special ice-cream event to thank their fans for their support, and a one-year anniversary party where they told Blinks they would make them proud and wanted the group and fans to stay together for ten or even twenty years.

SEVEN

JAPAN

apan is only 500 miles from South Korea, separated by the Sea of Japan, or the East Sea as the South Koreans call it. The two countries have much in common and yet their relationship is best described as 'it's complicated', with disputes arising from Japan's occupation of Korea in the first half of the twentieth century and territorial claims over a number of islands.

Many young people, however, eschew any traditional distrust of their neighbours across the sea, especially when it comes to art and culture. Japanese music, TV dramas and particularly anime have been popular in South Korea since the last cultural bans were lifted in the early twenty-first century. On the other side, the Land of the Rising Sun was one of the first countries to embrace *hallyu*, or the Korean Wave of pop culture, entertainment, music, TV dramas and movies.

YG and the other Korean entertainment companies were obviously eager to introduce their artists to this expanding audience, the world's second-largest music market after America. The youth of Japan love their music and have a voracious appetite for new sounds. Groups like TVXQ, Big Bang, SHINee and Girls' Generation became incredibly popular there and, although K-pop had experienced some quiet years, a new generation led by BTS and Twice (boasting three members of Japanese descent) had sparked new interest in acts from across the sea.

It would always have been part of YG's plan to send Blackpink to Japan early in their career. What no one expected was for the group to play their first solo concert outside Korea and across the sea. In May 2017, YG's official Japanese Twitter account announced they would not only be performing at the Nippon Budokan concert hall in Tokyo on 20 July, but they would also be releasing a Japanese-language mini-album on 9 August.

The Blackpink girls were not completely out of their depth in Japan. YG had made sure they had Japanese-language lessons; and, although Lisa still struggled to say very much (to be fair she was also learning Korean), the others had a good grasp of the language. It was Jennie who did a lot of the speaking in Japanese TV interviews, but many native speakers have credited Jisoo with having the better Japanese accent.

> It would always have been part of YG's plan to send Blackpink to Japan early in their career. What no one expected was for the group to play their first solo concert outside Korea and across the sea.

Earlier in the year, to introduce themselves to Japanese fans, the group had done a photoshoot and an interview for the Japanese edition of the magazine *Nylon*. There they spoke of their two-week stay in Japan as trainees, when they went out there for dance lessons. Rosé remarked on what a fun time they had and how they had all thought it would be good to live there for a while. Jennie proudly told them how she had named her dog Kuma – the Japanese for bear – as she thought the cute Pomeranian looked like a bear. For the photoshoot they wore Japanese designer outfits and they were excited to learn about and try out Japanese fashion. Lisa said she liked the light and charming make-up style, while Rosé listed the shopping areas and stores she was keen to visit: 'Shibuya, Harajuku, Omotesando and Don Quijote!'

In another interview, which appeared in Japanese street-fashion magazine *Zipper* in May, it was clear they were filled with anticipation about the trip, especially the shopping and eating. Rosé told how all the members loved Japanese food and at one time that was all they ate (Jennie picking out white-chocolate-covered strawberries as her favourite) and added, 'I want to go so badly that I'm speechless!'

The Nippon Budokan arena, a judo-arena-turned-concert-hall, holds 14,000 and a group with just a handful of songs could have found it a challenge to fill. However, reports suggested that there were enough applications for tickets to fill the venue twenty times over and Japan's sports newspapers, which all cover pop music, made Blackpink headline news, even if Nikkan Sports did call them 'Big Bang's younger sister'.

In anticipation of their arrival, YG had released Japanese music videos of the entire Blackpink back catalogue. These were pretty much identical to the previous versions except the lyrics were now all in Japanese, apart from the raps, which Jennie and Lisa delivered in English. This wasn't a great shock, as including English-language parts is common in Japanese versions of K-pop songs, but it certainly went down well with English-speaking and international fans.

On 20 July 2017 Blackpink were finally in the area and Japanese

Blinks were incredibly excited. Enthusiastic and armed with light sticks (even though the group were yet to release an official light stick), they made an awesome noise, even before the girls appeared on stage. The J-Blinks (Japanese fans) greeted every song with joy and produced the very first 'Pink Ocean' – a sea of pink light created by thousands of light sticks.

Later, the girls admitted they were extremely nervous as they waited for the stage to be raised to reveal them to the audience. Although this had been billed as their Japanese debut showcase, it was as near to a real concert as they had ever played; but it soon became clear that they were true performers – they looked great, sang clearly, danced on point and still made eye contact with the audience. Even more impressively, they were singing live in Japanese (and English).

The crowd immediately took them to their hearts – especially Lisa, who seemed to be greeted with extra warmth on every rap she performed – and the members all seemed genuinely astounded at the love and support they received from the J-Blinks. They began with 'Whistle' and 'Stay', before each of the members addressed the crowd in Japanese. After 'As If It's Your Last' they had a costume change before 'Boombayah' and 'Playing with Fire'. But the audience wouldn't let them finish there and, led by mascots Krunk (YG's bear mascot) and Hello Kitty, forced them to come back for an encore. This time they played the Korean version of 'Boombayah', dispensing with the choreography as they paraded around the edge of the stage, getting as close to the audience as possible in order to interact with them.

Playing an extended set in a concert hall was a brand-new experience for the girls. They later revealed how they felt so hot under the lights and the sweat ran into their eyes. Added to this, they were near to tears with the emotion of the experience and with being so close to their fans. They had to cope with a super-quick costume change mid-set and Lisa managed to swap her microphone with Jisoo, resulting in confusion in their earpiece playback.

A bigger problem was the stage. It looked fantastic, with purple, pink and blue lighting and a 360-degree revolving stage, but the platform was limited in size and for the early songs was raised to a few metres high. As a result, the girls, who were used to being as fierce as possible in their dance moves, had to hold back on their moves a little for fear of falling off the side. Such are the problems of live concert performances, but they were learning and clearly loving the experience. As Rosé said, halfway through the concert it had dawned on her: 'I am an actual singer. This is what an actual singer does!'

Blackpink were soon back on stage in Japan. At the beginning of August they were performing at the Hotto Motto Field Kobe stadium, which held an alarming 35,000 spectators, as they opened for Big Bang's Taeyang on two nights of his White Night world tour. This was an ideal opportunity not only to make new Japanese fans but also to gain experience of playing in a stadium without the pressure of being the main act.

Blackpink continued to focus attention on Japan through the summer of 2017, finally releasing their mini-album, titled *Blackpink*, on 29 August. The album included both Korean and Japanese versions of the releases to date. It went straight to number one in

> As Rosé said, halfway through the concert it had dawned on her: 'I am an actual singer. This is what an actual singer does!'

the Oricon (Japanese) album charts, putting Blackpink alongside Russian duo t.A.T.u. and their YG seniors 2NE1 as the only foreign groups to accomplish this feat with their debut album.

They performed 'Boombayah' live on Japanese TV, appearing in the morning on a news programme rather than a music show. Rosé in her tie-dye crop top and Jennie in a purple and black two-tone chiffon dress both caught attention and few seemed to notice Lisa's rap line being cut or the moment she and Jisoo bumped into each other (which they found very funny!) near the end of the dance. Lisa remarked on how different it was to performing on Korean TV, as the cameras were shooting from an altogether different angle.

Blackpink were also invited to perform at A-Nation, one of the biggest music festivals in Japan. The festival featured top Japanese artists as well as guest foreign acts. EXO and NCT 127 had appeared on the first day, with Blackpink and their friends iKON appearing the following day. Blackpink's short set of Japanese versions of their songs was enthusiastically received by the audience and those watching a livestream. Some noted a slight change of style, with minidresses replacing the shorts or pleated skirts that at least three of them usually wore – and indeed many commented that Lisa's marvellous swirling coloured dress was so tight and short it inhibited her dancing.

The girls had always been interested in Japanese fashion, but being in the country enabled them to immerse themselves in it. This was especially evident when they collaborated with *Nylon* magazine to help celebrate the

The September issue [of *Nylon*] had four limited-edition versions featuring each of the girls on a cover. It sold out in just three days.

tenth anniversary of the fashion brand Shel'tter. The September issue had four limited-edition versions featuring each of the girls on a cover. It sold out in just three days.

This was no surprise: the covers were fabulous, featuring the members dressed in super-trendy streetwear. All with varying shades of hair, from auburn to dark brown, and uncomplicated make-up, they each wore simple flat-coloured Moussy-branded clothes; Jisoo in a yellow T-shirt; Jennie in a long, baggy red shirt belted at the waist; Rosé in purple, with red and white striped collar; and Lisa in a long-sleeved green T-shirt. The poses, accessories and added touches were exquisite. Jisoo wore oversized glasses; Lisa, with eyeshadow perfectly matching her light-red hair, had the most luscious lips; Rosé's pale skin contrasted starkly with her dark eyes and hair; while in Jennie's shot, eyes were drawn to her pale-pink lips and thick chain earrings.

The Shel'tter store is located on the main street of Harajuku, Tokyo, the hub of Japanese fashion and culture. When a huge billboard featuring all four members was placed in the shop front it was clear that Blackpink had truly made an impression among Japanese fashion-watchers. This was reinforced at the end of summer, when they were invited to perform at two of Japan's biggest fashion events: the Tokyo Girls Collection and the Kobe Collection.

Blackpink's Japanese summer had been a roaring success. Their timing had been perfect as K-pop enjoyed a renaissance in the country and, though they had yet to reach the popularity of Twice or Big Bang, they were certainly ranked among Japanese music fans' top ten Korean acts. They had now performed at festivals and in stadiums, and J-Blinks, of which there were a growing number, had witnessed a solo Blackpink concert – something those at home, and around the world, were now dying to see for themselves.

EIGHT

BLACKPINK IN THE HOUSE

The ever-growing legions of new Blackpink fans soon learned a lesson that those who had followed the group since debut knew all too well: to be a Blink you needed patience. By autumn 2017, Blackpink had released just five tracks and were still to play a solo concert anywhere except Japan. Instead Blinks devoured Instagram posts of the group at airports or the photos that the girls enjoyed taking of one another, and they watched Blackpink YouTube videos on repeat and noticed the views steadily ticking over. Throughout 2017 their channel was averaging over 100 million views a month and by December 'As If It's Your Last' had become the fastest-ever K-pop group music video to reach 200 million views.

Their appearance on a new late-night music show in August was an instant YouTube favourite. Titled *Party People*, it was hosted by rival company JYP's boss, Park Jin-young, in a set that resembled an underground club. Blackpink appeared in the fourth episode of the series, performing their usual songs (looking ever more assured in a live setting) and joining their host at the bar to chat while sipping cocktails. They claimed it was the first time they'd had cocktails – and Jisoo spilled hers!

What really got the YouTube counters moving, though, were the other performances.

The show included a segment called 'Song I want to steal', which invited a guest to perform another artist's song. Blackpink's co-guest, the CNBlue singer Jung Yong-hwa, chose 'Playing with Fire' and performed his own acoustic version of it. Rosé was so taken with it she immediately invited him to join them at their next concert, but he had his own request: to hear her play guitar and sing a duet with him. Together they played an impromptu and beautiful duet of the Tamia hit 'Officially Missing You'.

If this wasn't enough, the show featured a new Blackpink song! Their own 'Song I want to steal' was 'Sure Thing', a 2010 US hit for Miguel; this was a cover in which all the lyrics were English. That wasn't a problem, with even Jisoo sounding like a native speaker in a rendition that left many open-mouthed: these girls had serious talent. The singing and harmonizing was spot on (with Jennie showing just how well she could sing when called upon to do so) and the performance included an extended rap break that Jennie and Lisa had written themselves. It was a revelation, winning over many doubters and even surprising Blinks who already thought the group was pretty awesome.

Even then *Party People* had one more Blackpink treat in store: a dance cover to Beyoncé's 'Partition'. Dressed all in black – similar to their dance-practice video outfits – and cheered on by a raucous crowd, the foursome worked through the edgy Kyle Hanagami choreography, full of grinding and body rolls. This was yet another performance that would go down in Blackpink history.

Blackpink's live act seemed to be getting better and better. In September, although not nominated, they appeared as special guests at the MTV Music Video Awards Japan, treating the audience to 'Boombayah' and 'As If It's Your Last'. Their performance was acclaimed by some as sensational and by most as one of the highlights of a star-studded evening.

Returning to Korea for festival season, they took to the stage at the Korea Music Festival, the Fever Festival and others, each time receiving a rapturous reception. Meanwhile, online chat focused on rumours that they were working on a new track and (soon to be verified by airport photos) that Jisoo was now sporting jet-black hair and bangs – a look that went down very well with Blinks.

> While Blinks waited for the new song, they were briefly distracted in November when the 'As If It's Your Last' music video was featured in the US superhero movie *Justice League*.

While Blinks waited for the new song, they were briefly distracted in November when the 'As If It's Your Last' music video was featured in the US superhero movie *Justice League*. In the movie Bruce Wayne (Batman), played by Ben Affleck, has broken into the high-tech den of the Flash. When the Scarlet Speedster discovers him there, the video is playing on one of the monitors with the sound system blasting out the sweet Blackpink sound. Ezra Miller, the Hollywood star who plays the Flash, delighted fans even further when he admitted to being a Blackpink fan himself. He was soon made an honorary Blink and was presented with a CD autographed by the whole group. It would be a while before he met any of them, but in September 2019 he was pictured with Rosé at the Saint Laurent fashion show at Paris Fashion Week.

If there was one thing Blinks desired as much as a comeback, it was a reality series – so YG's YouTube teaser video in November 2017 was a godsend. It showed the members of Blackpink being set up by their company around the time of their anniversary in August. The secret-camera-style prank featured a pretend interview in which they gave a list of wishes to their boss. They said how he'd promised them a reality show and to give them new furniture and that they'd like a holiday and to shop with his credit card. Then YG's boss emerged with an anniversary cake and, like a fairy godfather, revealed that their wishes were about to come true with a '100cation' – a 100-day holiday. Blinks were already excited and they still had two months before the show would be broadcast. Meanwhile, the girls were packing their bags ...

Blinks were so amped for the forthcoming show that it made up for their idols not appearing at the MMAs or MAMAs, the two major pre-Christmas award events (Blackpink were nominated but failed to pick up an award at the shows). And they soon had more exciting news: the group were scheduled to appear on a TV special on Christmas Day. The 2017 *Gayo Daejun* was the twentieth year of this televised musical extravaganza, which had become a Christmas tradition featuring the best K-pop acts around. Alongside Blackpink, this year's event at the massive Gocheok Sky Dome in Seoul saw Twice, Red Velvet, BTS, EXO, NCT 127 and virtually other every big name feature in the line-up.

The theme of the 2017 show was bands who had had number one hits during the year performing covers, and Blackpink duly took on the 2007 hit 'So Hot' by Wonder Girls – a tribute to the ground-breaking girl group that had disbanded earlier in the year. To a track especially rearranged by Teddy, the girls re-energized the song by giving it the Blackpink treatment. They dialled up the girl-crush confidence and added their own rap part, including the now iconic line in which they boast about being the only gang to run the game in high heels.

The group sashayed and strutted on the massive stage in their trademark elegant but sexy outfits. Jennie was in a sheer lacy black top with braces and a velvet skirt; Rosé wore a black sparkly crop top with a split short white skirt; Lisa sported a white crop top with silk puff shoulders and gold brocaded black shorts; and Jisoo, her black hair in a ponytail, had a feathered white top and black bow at the neck, heavy-duty earrings and tight black shorts. There was no mistaking what they were conveying in their dance, outfits and song. These were assertive women with style and attitude. They were gorgeous and they knew it.

> They dialled up the girl-crush confidence and added their own rap part, including the now iconic line in which they boast about being the only gang to run the game in high heels.

That same evening saw a studio recording of the track drop, titled 'So Hot – the Black Label remix' (Black Label was a YG sub-label run by Teddy and another YG producer, Kush). It was released on YouTube and the free streaming platform SoundCloud, and within fifteen hours it had already hit the 2 million views mark on YouTube. That was some Christmas present for the ever-loyal Blinks.

Now it was just a two-week wait for *Blackpink House*. A dedicated reality series was a must-have for any K-pop group on the up. Seventeen's island challenges on *One Fine Day*, BTS's Scandinavian trip on *Bon Voyage* and Winner's *Youth over Flowers*, an Australian survival series, were great examples of how they could bring fans and groups together. There wasn't to be too much hardship for Blackpink, though, as they were only going as far as central Seoul. They were to stay in a specially prepared 'Pink Princess House' in the hip and cool neighbourhood of Hongdae. Survival wouldn't be an issue, but they did have to do all their own cooking, cleaning and washing. In return, though, they would receive an all-expenses-paid holiday.

The series was called *Blackpink House* in honour of the fabulous apartment, but before we saw that we got our first real look around their dorm as the group members selected their outfits for the 100cation. Although each of them have their own room, the furnishing is basic and you can see how four people living there together might feel a little cramped. Their Princess Palace was altogether more lavish. A pink-tiled white building with a pink neon sign reading 'All-Day In The Pink' on an adjacent building, it had a sparkling kitchen, a spacious living area, luxurious bedrooms and even a special video-game room for Jisoo.

Over a few months, through eleven sixty-minute episodes, Blinks got to know their idols better than ever. As well as enjoying their luxury house, they travelled to Thailand (where Lisa acted as their guide), were seen preparing for a concert in Yokohama in Japan, and visited the Korean holiday destination Jeju Island. Back in Seoul they were kept busy with anything from preparing a hundred sandwiches for a guerrilla fan meet and surprising Jisoo on her last day as MC on *Inkigayo* to accompanying Rosé on a magazine photoshoot and filming an alternative video for 'Boombayah'.

Fans have so many great memories from *Blackpink House*. There was Jennie giving Jisoo a back hug; the four of them trying *aegyo* and dancing in order to get a discount at a furniture store; the moment when Lisa had a surprise – and highly emotional – meeting with her parents in Thailand; Lisa and Rosé's in-bed exercise routine; Jisoo taking Dalgomie to the training centre; sleeping Jennie being literally dragged out of bed; Jennie and Lisa's uncontrollable laughter as their manager failed at the bowling alley; Jisoo's helium song at their Christmas party; and Lisa's joy at receiving her Secret Santa present.

Through surprises, challenges, games, adventures and simply hanging out together, *Blackpink House* revealed just how funny, cute and, in a way, ordinary the four girls were – and how much they enjoyed eating! Most of all it confirmed how close they had grown, as seen in their touching letters to each other in the final episode. After all, they had spent six years together as trainees and undergone an intense eighteen months since their debut. It had clearly forged deep bonds and Blinks were constantly assessing who was closer, devising their own names for friendships – Jensoo (Jennie and Jisoo), Chaesoo (Jisoo and Rosé), Lisoo (Lisa and Jisoo), Chaennie (Jennie and Rosé), Jenlisa (Jennie and Lisa) and Chaelisa (Rosé and Lisa) – but fan discussions were long and inconclusive, really proving only that all four felt completely comfortable in each other's company.

Blackpink House marked the end of another incredible year for the group. They had released just one new single and yet they had gone from strength

> *Blackpink House* revealed just how funny, cute and, in a way, ordinary the four girls were – and how much they enjoyed eating!

to strength. They had won over legions of new fans in Japan, shown their charisma in their own reality series and continued to impress with their live performances. They had also established themselves as individual talents, with Jisoo presenting on TV, Rosé winning plaudits for her guitar playing and singing, Lisa modelling for Nanogen and Jennie being chosen as the new model for Chanel Beauty. All Blinks needed now was a comeback.

NINE

FAIR AND SQUARE

K-pop fans have a special term for acts that go more than a few months without touring or promoting new releases. They say the company is keeping them in their 'dungeon'. Of course, Blinks were not really suggesting that YG had locked Blackpink up in some subterranean cell in their Seoul headquarters (or they'd have broken them out, for sure!), but such language was seen more frequently as 2018 began. The truth was, even if they were not promoting, the girls were busier than ever, with magazine shoots, filming *Blackpink House*, performances at awards shows and their solo ventures, but still they kept in touch with their Blinks via regular posts on Twitter and the group Instagram account, as well as through their V Live broadcasts.

Blackpink's V Live channel was proving particularly popular, with the girls' sweet nature, humour and honesty appealing to fans around the world. In February, for the first time, they were named among the app's top ten channels alongside other giants of K-pop. The statistics confirmed that most Blackpink fans came from South-East Asia, with Thailand, the Philippines and Indonesia topping the list of countries with most viewers. Only then came

South Korea, with Vietnam, the USA, Brazil, Mexico and Malaysia also placing high.

By then, a seemingly casual comment had caused excitement among Blinks around the globe. On Instagram, the YG supremo replied to a fan's complaint about the lack of recordings by saying it was indeed ridiculous that Blackpink had released only one new song last year and that they were working to put that right – on the previous evening they had apparently been at the studio until midnight. He explained that they were working on a mini-album, but, asking for just a little more patience, could not yet give a release date. Nearly two months later, in another Instagram post, he uploaded a pink square, hashtagged #Blackpink, and confirmed that they were 'Done With Recording'.

While Blinks guessed when they might hear the results, Blackpink carried on working. They were back in Japan where their profile was boosted by appearing in a TV ad for Puma Suede Bow shoes and they performed at the prestigious Sukkiri Super Live concert. They appeared in a Sprite advert back in Korea and at Myongji University Festival in the middle of May. There, Jisoo and Lisa both showed off their new shorter haircuts – such a change was a good sign that a comeback was happening!

As May drew to a close, not only was the comeback date – 15 June – finally revealed, but news also broke that Blinks were to finally get their own light stick. Talk about a double whammy! Every major K-pop group has to have their own light stick, a handheld, 20–30 cm battery-powered LED light specially designed to represent the act. It gives fans the opportunity to show their allegiance to their idols and to be part of the group's performances, and when held aloft by thousands of fans light sticks create an awesome ocean of colour.

Blackpink had been involved in the design process for their light stick, which they called the 'hammer-bong'. They were inspired by the joke hammers used by *Weekly Idol* hosts Jeong Hyeong-don and Defconn, and helped come up with the concept of a black handle with a double head made up of two pink hearts. It had settings that enabled it to be used as a squeaky hammer or a responsive mode that enabled the light stick to react to music. Just like the girls, it was smart, sweet and silly with a hint of menace!

In the first two weeks of June 2018 the excitement levels rose due to a series of teasers: moving posters, snippets of audio and an album photo poster that featured the girls in close-up with a red tint. Jennie caught the attention with her wavy hair, face gems and divine crescent-moon-print stretch jersey top, and Lisa looked every inch a pop star in her black and white chequered top, ruby-red lipstick and black leather choker. But it was the photo of Jisoo that really set tongues wagging. Although the soft, red haze made it hard to work out the colours, she had a light, short bob and her bangs fell over her eyebrows. She looked simply sensational.

[The hammer-bong] had settings that enabled it to be used as a squeaky hammer or a responsive mode that enabled the light stick to react to music. Just like the girls, it was smart, sweet and silly with a hint of menace!

Square Up was released on 15 June, with Blackpink holding a press conference and then a special V Live broadcast to introduce the new mini-album. Over 850,000 viewers logged on to hear them say how they'd upped the intensity and glamour, with the added bonus of Lisa announcing the comeback in five different languages! That evening, the four members launched their own individual Instagram accounts. Jennie was @jennierubyjane, Rosé was @roses_are_rosie, Jisoo was @sooyaaa__ and Lisa was @lalalalisa_m. Each of them posted the same image – of the four of them in exaggerated poses with Lisa doing a cartwheel – and linked to the others' accounts. By the end of the day they had all surpassed 1 million followers.

The mini-album contained four tracks, including the lead single 'Ddu-du Ddu-du'. While the other tracks had been produced a while ago, the single had only recently been put together by Teddy. The girls and YG had chosen to promote it as they believed it was the most powerful of their songs and demonstrated the upfront character of the group. It took just a few seconds to get dragged into the song as the distorted synth whistle sounded out. This penetrating riff, together with the strident vocals and rap, carried the song, with background beats, a booming bass, guitars and Indian-sounding chords sweeping in and out. With trademark Blackpink elements like a chant, machine-gun-style repeated (English) words and a fun chorus, there was little doubt they had a hit on their hands.

For the first time the song seemed to be built around the rap parts rather than just using them for variety and texture. Jennie and Lisa really put it out there, but the song was about self-belief and the solid strength of Rosé and Jisoo's vocals was also essential. The lyrics find Blackpink reiterating that they are super-confident, strong and keeping it real – and they don't care what anyone thinks. There are girl-power lines, nonsense lyrics and pure-fun phrases, but they all come together because each member expresses attitude and energy superbly.

The accompanying video totally reflected the group and the song. It is magnificently opulent, and oozes glamour and power while incorporating some superb dance moves and a dash of their trademark humour. These are girls in control – whether it is Rosé, high on a pedestal; Lisa wielding a Blackpink katana (samurai sword); Jennie sitting eating popcorn on a tank; or Jisoo, standing in the midst of destruction yet indestructible under her umbrella. The four members play their parts to perfection, too. The swag is turned up to eleven and they pout and stare, daring you to judge them, but there are also the reminders – Rosé looking up at herself on the pedestal, Jisoo tripping up in front of the huge mural – that they are ordinary people, not actual goddesses.

> Chanel, Dolce & Gabbana, Balmain, Saint Laurent – the video is a smorgasbord of stylish and beautiful high-end fashion.

Of course, the whole thing looks great, too. The colour is full-on, with pink and black to the fore, and the sets and effects are extravagant, from the life-size chessboard to the pink-dollar-bill rain to the massive chandelier swing and diamond-encrusted tank. As for the outfits, the expectation was that these girls would go glam for a video, but this was off the scale. The shoot featured thousands of dollars' worth of haute couture, designer streetwear and jewellery. Chanel, Dolce & Gabbana, Balmain, Saint Laurent – the video is a smorgasbord of stylish and beautiful high-end fashion, and it demands repeated viewing to pick out the details and take it all in.

The girls' looks – crop tops, minidresses, tight shorts, boots – come together in the dance sections, but the video also features each of them as individuals. Jennie is first up, sitting on her throne in her Dolce & Gabbana rainbow gown. Her image is chic and pretty, typified by the Vivienne Westwood plaid jacket and large orb pedant, but she can also do fun, with a purple ponytail or oversized Jacquemus wide-brim hat. Lisa is the edgy hip-hop temptress in a pink Dior suit, US Nascar jacket and spiked leather pumps or thigh-high, turquoise Y/Project boots. Rosé is the most classically feminine, whether in a black tulle minidress, Saint Laurent flower-decorated sandals or the Alexander McQueen black and red ruffled stretch-knit dress she wears on the swing (at nearly $4,000, this was said to be the single most expensive piece worn in the video), while Jisoo manages to defy such categories, wearing anything from a Paco Rabanne gold sports bra to a classy YSL floral and gold lamé playsuit. And just who else could pull off a pink-with-dark-roots bob wig?

Packed with symbolism and cryptic delights (such as Lisa's blackboard, which contained a myriad of information, from members' signatures and their training dates to their music-video view counts), the video trended at number one on YouTube almost immediately, reaching 10 million views within six hours and 20 million views after just thirteen hours. After a day it had made history as the most-viewed K-pop video on YouTube within its first twenty-four hours. The success was more than the group ever expected. 'We were actually very nervous,' Rosé later admitted. 'Because of our year-long break, we were worried that we might have been forgotten.'

At the same time, *Square Up* was topping forty or so album charts around the world and fans were getting to hear more Blackpink music. 'Forever Young' was the favourite of the other three tracks on the album; a summer bop with a reggaeton and tropical house-influenced rhythm, a catchy chorus and an extended rap and dance break. It was also impossible to miss the repeated line 'Blackpink is the revolution', something Blinks immediately took to heart.

The next track, 'Really', was also a gem. It takes the tempo down a little, but still flows along contagiously. Here Rosé's vocals maintain the sweetness levels, Jisoo raps for the first time, like she's been doing it all her life, and the whole song brims with character. 'See U Later', the last track on the mini-album, takes them back to the fast beats and the badass attitude in a monumental dumping song that sees the girls chew over and spit out a series of witty and caustic put-downs. This is where they completely nail the black side of Blackpink. You wouldn't want to mess with them in this mood!

By the time Blackpink held their comeback stage, performing 'Ddu-du Ddu-du' and 'Forever Young' on *Show! Music Core* on 16 June and *Inkigayo* the following day, *Square Up* was already a certified success. Blackpink were the most viewed group globally on YouTube and the video had notched up 5 million views. In Korea, the album and single shot to number one. *Square Up* was the best-selling debut album by a girl group and 'Ddu-du Ddu-du' achieved a rare 'perfect all-kill', reaching number one in all domestic charts.

The international response was even more breathtaking. It went to number one on the iTunes Worldwide Album chart and the Billboard World Albums chart, but also did amazingly well in Japan, New Zealand, Canada, Switzerland, France and the UK (where 'Ddu-du Ddu-du' went to seventy-eight in the singles chart). The US had seriously woken up to Blackpink, too. *Square Up* reached number forty and became the highest-peaking album on the Billboard 200 by a Korean girl group, while the single matched that record by reaching number fifty-five, having got to twenty-three on the iTunes chart. Whichever way you looked at it, Blackpink were slaying it and they were a worldwide phenomenon.

In their comeback stages and the dance-practice video that was soon released, fans were able to see the full choreography. The dance is a series of smooth moves punctuated by body rolls and hair flicks. It is full of swagger and physical contact, often turning the four girls into one unit, but it is best remembered for its iconic chorus section, where the girls energetically use their hands as guns. 'I think the point of it is to be savage, get out your guns and hit 'em with it,' Rosé later told esteemed American music magazine *Billboard*. 'Show them your jawline,' she added, 'and maybe your highlighter.'

In the summer of 2018, pretty much wherever you were in the world, there was no avoiding 'Ddu-du Ddu-du'. Over the next few weeks, promoting it widely on the Korean music shows, Blackpink picked up a mighty eleven trophies. It was by no means a record, but it put the song alongside 'Gangnam Style', 'Fake Love' and 'Call Me Baby' as one of TV viewers' favourite tracks of recent years. And even when they finished promoting 'Ddu-du Ddu-du', Blackpink spent the rest of July on 'Forever Young', performing the fierce choreography on a number of shows.

As the promotion came to a close, YG made good on a promise. During the broadcast of *Blackpink House*, the company had said a twelfth episode would be released if the series surpassed 88 million views on YouTube and V Live. Blinks had amassed this total back in March, but once again had had to wait patiently for their bonus episode. It eventually appeared in mid-August, but was worth the wait. The episode took viewers behind the scenes of Blackpink's comeback, from the university festival performances, shooting the video and filming their dance practice to their first comeback stage. Many fans believed it to be the best yet, as it showed Blackpink's working life rather than just the fun challenges.

Such unprecedented exposure to Blackpink eventually had to come to an end – unless you were in Japan. No sooner had the group finished promoting 'Forever Young' than they set off for their first-ever solo tour, a seven-show arena tour across Osaka, Fukuoka and Chiba, with all 80,000 tickets selling out within a couple of days. With the songs from *Square Up* as well as the Japanese versions of their previous recordings, the group now had enough for a full concert. However, the J-Blinks were to be spoiled with not only these, 'So Hot' and the Beyoncé 'Partition' dance, but also a number of solo covers. Jennie sang Frankie Valli's 1960s US hit 'Can't Take My Eyes Off You'; Rosé covered Halsey's 'Eyes Closed' and Taeyang's K-pop smash 'Eyes, Nose, Lips' (accompanying herself on guitar); Lisa danced to Rihanna's 'Lemon', 'Faded' by Tink and Charlie Puth's 'Attention'; and Jisoo went the extra mile to please the local fans by singing 'Sakurairo Mau Koro', a 2005 hit for Japanese star Mika Nakashima.

> No sooner had the group finished promoting 'Forever Young' than they set off for their first-ever solo tour, a seven-show arena tour across Osaka, Fukuoka and Chiba, with all 80,000 tickets selling out within a couple of days.

In the Japanese arena tour In Your Area (the tour name was chosen by fans), Blackpink proved they had the stagecraft, stamina, charisma and material to thrill their fans. In fact, they were proving so popular in Japan that they had already scheduled their first dome concert at the 50,000-seater Kocera Dome in Osaka on Christmas Eve. Meanwhile, fans were still waiting for the girls' first full concert on home territory. Their patience was finally rewarded in September when two dates in November at the Olympic Gymnastics Arena in Seoul were announced. With both dates selling out in a matter of minutes, Blinks were officially excited.

TEN

COLLABORATING AND GOING SOLO

t was, as the reputable business magazine *Forbes* wrote, 'An East-meets-West summit between international It Girls'. While Blackpink represented the Eastern hemisphere in this collaboration, the West had one of the hottest talents around in Dua Lipa. Blackpink (especially Jennie, who said that the English star's 'New Rules' was her favourite-ever song) had been long-time fans of the singer and when their idol brought her tour to Seoul in May 2018, Jennie and Lisa not only had front-row circle seats but also met up with her after the show.

Desperate for a collaboration, international K-pop fans in particular jump on any interaction between Western stars and their favourites, but successful link-ups are rare. However, this meeting between girls of the same age and musical interests bore fruit. 'I was just like, "Oh my God, would it be crazy if I just sent them a song and just see if they liked it and want to sing on it?"' Lipa later revealed. 'They were like, "Yeah, let's do it!"' Dua Lipa had written 'Kiss and Make Up' a year before and was hoping to record it for her second album; having met Blackpink, though,

> ['Kiss and Make Up'] enabled Blackpink to become the first-ever female K-pop group to enter the Official UK Top 40 and became their second song to enter the US Billboard Hot 100.

she decided it would be perfect as a collaboration for the deluxe reissue of her debut album. Soon they were busy exchanging messages, with the girls changing some of the English lyrics to Korean.

The result was an electro-dance track in which Dua Lipa's rasping voice slots in perfectly alongside the Blackpink voices (with no rap parts – all of them had vocal lines). It was almost like she was a fifth member of the group! 'Kiss and Make Up' was released in October 2018 and it was no surprise when it reached number one on iTunes in Indonesia, the Philippines, Thailand and Singapore and across South-East Asia – but eyebrows were also raised in the West. The track enabled Blackpink to become the first-ever female K-pop group to enter the Official UK Top 40 and became their second song to enter the US Billboard Hot 100.

The single was the perfect primer for the group's first solo concerts at the home of K-pop, Seoul. On 10 November 2018 they took to the stage in front of 10,000 ecstatic fans at the Olympic Gymnastics Arena. The girls all seemed to be thrilled to be playing in their adopted home town, giving their all as they went through their repertoire, as well as stopping to address the assembled Blinks and have a little fun teasing each other. Performing in front of a live band and dancing with full intensity, they put in so much effort they were notably out of breath after some songs. This was particularly true after their exciting new group-dance performance to Stefflon Don's '16 Shots' (in which Rosé's amazing hair flicks became a real talking point).

The second part of the show once again saw them showcase their individual talents. Rosé, this time without the guitar, stunned the crowd with her vocal ability as she performed The Beatles' 'Let It Be', 'You and I', a song by Park Bom from 2NE1, and Big Bang singer Taeyang's 'Only Look at Me'. Lisa, backed by the YG dancers Crazy Girls, danced to Cardi B's 'I Like It' and Charlie Puth's 'Attention', but it was her hot duet dance with Dony, a male dancer from YG's Kwon Twins, that really raised the roof. Jisoo then covered 'Clarity'; the original singer, Zedd, responded with a heart-eyes emoji when he saw a fan's video clip of the performance on Twitter.

The crowd guessed what was coming next. YG had recently announced that each of the Blackpink members would be releasing solo recordings and Jennie was first up with a track, appropriately titled 'Solo', that would be premiered at the Seoul concert. Now the audience not only got to see the video first but they then welcomed Jennie as she strolled out wearing a beautiful red and black sequin and lace bustier over an off-the-shoulder white blouse, just as she had worn in the dance scene in the video, and proceeded to show she had the stage presence and talent to carry off a fabulous solo performance.

If Jennie was exhausted by the two Seoul concerts, she had little time to recuperate. The very next day, 12 November, saw the release of 'Solo'. It was written and produced by Teddy Park and it was no surprise that it had the hallmarks of a Blackpink song, with the synth riff, finger-snapping beat and a catchy chorus built around the 'lo-lo-lo' repetition. His minimalist approach gave Jennie a great opportunity to make the song her own through her vocals and rap, and she rose to the occasion, portraying the emotion and steel in the story of a young woman revelling in her freedom after ending a toxic relationship.

Jennie had gone all the way to London to shoot the video, a series of beautiful vignettes that echo the story, with Jennie looking fabulous whether brooding in the bay window of a stylish mansion, contemplative in a launderette or smiling in her angel wings as she rides in an open-topped car. She looked more stunning than ever, her hair varying from unkempt to a top knot to centre-parted and tied tight flamenco-style. The blue eyeshadow in the pool scene was striking and the peach in the garden was sumptuous. Of course, there was also an extensive list of beautiful and expensive outfits, headed by her Saks Potts bright-blue fur jacket, a super-comfy Burberry-motif cashmere jacket, the off-white ruffled mesh gown she wears in the garden and, naturally, being Jennie, the Chanel swimsuit.

'Solo' was an immediate all-kill on eight different music charts in Korea. It topped iTunes charts in forty different countries and surpassed 10 million views on YouTube in one day. After twenty-three days it had passed 100 million views, making her the fastest female Korean solo artist to reach that milestone – and she had already made history as the first solo female K-pop act to top Billboard's World Digital Song Sales chart as a lead artist. Add three victories on *Inkigayo*, despite being up against K-pop giants in Twice, Wanna One, BtoB and Red Velvet, and 'Solo' was surely a bigger hit than anyone could have imagined. YG promised Rosé was next in line for a solo and now Blinks just couldn't wait.

It may seem surprising that, with the success of 'Ddu-du Ddu-du', 'Solo' and the In Your Area tour, Blackpink still failed to take home a major prize (*daesang*) at the end-of-year awards shows. There were many possible explanations for the disappointment, such as the vagaries of the voting system, YG's relationship with the organizers and the lack of releases, but increasingly it seemed that the Korean public did not *get* the group quite as much as international K-pop fans did. A survey of which countries streamed the group most on YouTube listed the top ten as: Indonesia, Thailand, the Philippines, Vietnam, Brazil, USA, Malaysia, Mexico, Turkey and Japan.

Before the year was over, Blackpink headed back out to Japan, where they played a Christmas Eve concert at the Kyocera Dome in Osaka. It was not only their first Dome performance but also the first time an overseas girl group had played the massive 50,000-capacity venue. The set followed the pattern of the recent concerts with a solo section, in which Jisoo covered a different Mika Nakashima song, 'Yuki No Hana', taking them up to the interval. When the girls reappeared, the audience squealed with delight. It wasn't Blackpink's style for all four members to wear the same outfits, but here they all were dressed identically – in sexy Santa costumes!

As they began dancing to the festive classic 'Jingle Bell Rock', fans soon realized they were re-creating the famous high-school talent-show performance from the hit movie *Mean Girls* (even down to the dance mix-up, which saw Lisa push Jisoo as she pretended to get it wrong). Just like in the movie, the music suddenly cut out, but

Before the year was over, Blackpink headed back out to Japan, where they played a Christmas Eve concert at the Kyocera Dome in Osaka. It was not only their first Dome performance but also the first time an overseas girl group had played the massive 50,000- capacity venue.

instead of the Plastics' a cappella performance the song moved up in tempo and the girls broke into some fierce dance moves. They followed this up with a Japanese-language version of 'Rudolph the Red Nose Reindeer' and then, sitting on steps of the stage, sang Wham!'s 'Last Christmas', sharing out the vocal lines. Later in the show the fans turned the tables, surprising the members as they raised heart-shaped signs with the line 'Blackpink and Blink, we are forever'. The girls were moved to tears at such an outpouring of affection.

The very next day, Christmas Day, Blackpink were back at Gocheok Sky Dome for the 2018 *SBS Gayo Daejun* TV special. They had wowed the crowd at the red-carpet event, turning heads in their outfits from Alexander McQueen's new collection – Jennie in a mesh patchwork knit dress, Rosé sporting a red and white floral minidress, Jisoo wearing a sheer red lace dress and Lisa in a cropped leather biker jacket. Except for Lisa, all the members also wore different versions of McQueen's distinctive black leather corsets. All in all, it added up to a cool $30,000 worth of haute couture.

Their performance at the show created even more waves and is still regarded as one of their greatest ever, with the official YouTube video already amassing over 100 million views. Everything was spot-on: the black outfits embellished with silver (this time Jisoo was the exception in swirling shiny mauve and yellow), the choreography and especially the transitions between songs. Jennie began their section with her 'Solo' stage, but as she entered the dance finale the other members rose to appear from nowhere to join her. Seamlessly they then moved into 'Ddu-du Ddu-du' and finally headed to the front stage to finish with 'Forever Young'. Receiving rave reviews for their performance, Blackpink had managed to end a year in which they had achieved so much with one more high.

Blinks had good reason to be excited about 2019, but few expected the news that hit on 1 January. Every country has its own special New Year traditions, but over the past few years South Korea has developed a new one. Since 2013 the Korean news agency *Dispatch* has celebrated New Year's Day by revealing secret celebrity couples to the public. This year it disclosed that since the previous October Jennie had been dating Kai from the superstar boy band EXO. The two idols had been snapped on a late-night drive-and-park date in Seoul and it was reported that Kai even uploaded photos that Jennie had taken to his Instagram account. EXO's company, SM Entertainment, quickly confirmed that they were officially dating and added, 'They have good feelings towards each other.'

It was not the first time K-pop couples had been revealed, but these were the two biggest stars to have been linked. Romantic relationships can be a tricky issue in K-pop; in the past, entertainment companies had clamped down on their idols dating, even putting clauses in their contracts that prohibited them from any affairs. Fans had also been known to react adversely, even campaigning for the idol to be thrown out of the group. However, times change and companies' and fans' attitudes have become much more relaxed. Most Blinks (and EXO-Ls) celebrated the news and took great pleasure in spotting Kai and Jennie's 'couple items', such as scarves, sneakers

> [*Dispatch*] disclosed that since the previous October Jennie had been dating Kai from the superstar boy band EXO.

and beanies. Some went further and discovered that both Kai and Jennie had travelled to Paris and posted individual pics in front of the Eiffel Tower in early October. Jennie's caption even read, 'Had the most romantic dinner admiring the eiffel [*sic*] tower' with the hashtag #happyjen.

For all the stories of jealous fans or over-protective entertainment companies, the main reason that K-pop idols don't date is that there simply isn't time for romance in their busy schedules. Finding a moment for a romantic rendezvous between promoting, preparing new songs, practising choreography, touring and modelling engagements is difficult enough without having to evade press cameras and the well-meaning fans of two of the biggest groups in the country. Blinks and EXO-Ls were therefore not completely surprised when SM Entertainment subsequently announced that the pair had decided to end their relationship because of the pressures of work. However, it didn't stop them hoping that the couple might get back together again in the future.

'Ddu-du Ddu-du' became the fastest-ever K-pop music video to reach 600 million views.

And there was no denying Blackpink were busy. They were back performing at the Sky Dome in the first week of the year at the Golden Disc Awards. They picked up a *bonsang* (an award for the best ten songs of the year) and also a new award, the Cosmopolitan Artist Award, which they shared with boy band Wanna One. This recognition of the group's international appeal was reinforced on 12 January when 'Ddu-du Ddu-du' became the fastest-ever K-pop music video to reach 600 million views.

Blackpink now took the In Your Area tour around South-East Asia, visiting Thailand, Indonesia and Hong Kong. Everywhere they played they performed their set with the same energy as they had done in Seoul, engaged with the audience and went down a storm. The visit to Bangkok in January 2019 was particularly special as it was a homecoming for Lisa. Here her solo set included an electric dance performance to Jason Derulo's 'Swalla'. A fan-filmed clip of her dance soon went viral, racking up over 5 million views in a couple of days. Among those who viewed it was Jason Derulo himself, who retweeted the clip to his own followers. The girls were winning over new fans in the West every day and it was in that direction that they would soon set their sights.

ELEVEN

WELCOME TO AMERICA

There's one talent necessary for any K-pop idol that often goes unnoticed: you've got to be able to keep a secret. Back in the summer of 2018, when Blackpink were promoting 'Ddu-du Ddu-du', they had a visit from Paul Tollett, organizer of Coachella Festival. He flew all the way to South Korea to personally invite the group to play at the 2019 event. Over a period of twenty years, Coachella, which takes place near Palm Springs in California, has become one of the world's most prestigious festivals, attracting around 250,000 people. Blackpink were not only going to join such stars as Ariana Grande, Janelle Monáe and The 1975 on the bill, but would also be the festival's first-ever K-pop girl group. And they couldn't tell anyone for six months!

The news was finally revealed as the group set off for the final leg of their In Your Area tour of South-East Asia, playing sold-out arenas and stadiums in Manila in the Philippines, Singapore, Kuala Lumpur in Malaysia and Taipei in Taiwan. At every concert vast swathes of Blinks, nearly all dressed in black and pink, would light up the hall with their hammer-bong light sticks. For their part the girls went through every set with the enthusiasm of a first performance as they demonstrated their dancing prowess, vocal abilities, amazing costumes, sweet charm and unbelievable stamina.

However, Jennie, Rosé, Lisa and Jisoo are, of course, too much fun for every concert to be the same. They would try out lines in the local language, talk to fans about their city, lead the Mexican waves and have plenty of laughs with each other. In Singapore, Lisa passed her mic to Rosé to finish her rap part in 'Ddu-du Ddu-du', which Rosé duly delivered like a natural. The ace vocalist then returned the favour, making Lisa finish her high note, which she also performed impeccably, like the pro she is.

At the end of each performance fans and the members would come together, all joining in an emotional rendition of 'Stay', which had now become the Blinks' anthem. At this point the Blackpink girls came to the front of the stage to interact with the fans, talking to some and pointing out or even collecting their favourite posters and banners. In Manila, Rosé noticed a fan holding a plushie that had her baby photo over its face. 'This is so cute,' she squealed. 'You guys are so creative.' Fans then revealed plushies with the other members' baby faces on them and to everyone's excitement the group posed with their 'baby selves' at the front of the stage.

In between the Manila and Singapore concerts, Blackpink made their US debut in a whirlwind but memorable trip. As they flew out to LA on 7 February 2019 Blinks made sure that #HereComesBLACKPINK was trending at the very top of the worldwide Twitter rankings. The girls didn't have much time to explore, but made time for a shopping trip to Santa Monica. 'It was supposed to be for fashion,' Jennie told *Billboard*; but, admitting they had mistakenly expected California to be warm in February, she added, 'We ended up just grabbing anything that was warm.'

The reason Blackpink were in LA was to be introduced by Universal Music Group (their US company) at the label's pre-Grammy Awards showcase. Their US debut took place on 9 February inside a small tent in downtown Los Angeles, in front of an invite-only audience of around 400 music-business executives. Nevertheless, they still gave it their all, performing 'Ddu-du Ddu-du' and 'Forever Young', and making a number of previously casually interested attendees sit up and take notice.

The following day (wrapped up in warm clothes) they were back at the airport en route to New York for a US TV blitz. Rosé would celebrate her twenty-second birthday with just her three closest friends at an Italian restaurant in the Big Apple in between appearances on *The Late Show with Stephen Colbert*, *Strahan and Sara* and *Good Morning America*. In interviews they were sweet and charming (especially Rosé, who is the least shy English speaker), while in performance they were fierce and completely on it. The highlight was their appearance in *Good Morning America*'s Times Square studio. US Blinks, some of whom had waited all night in the cold in order to catch a glimpse of the group, packed the studio to see them perform live and hear them announce that, in addition to the Coachella dates, they had scheduled a North American tour to take place in April and May.

> Blackpink had become the first K-pop girl group to grace [*Billboard*'s] cover.

Blackpink had spent only a few days in the USA, but they were getting plenty of attention. The March edition of *Billboard* came out shortly after they returned to their tour in Singapore and Blackpink had become the first K-pop girl group to grace the magazine's cover. The headline read, 'Blackpink Meets the Red,

White and Blue' with a line underneath saying, 'After years training for US domination, K-pop's new queens finally touch down.'

Not only were the four girls on the magazine's pink-hued front cover, but four alternative single-member covers were also available. In the main image, they were all lying on their backs, heads together, looking up at the camera, with their long hair splayed out behind them. The blondes, Lisa and Rosé, lay next to each other with Jisoo next to Jennie, fingers intertwined. There was strong colour in Jennie's yellow and black bustier check dress and Jisoo's blue brocade dress (and Lisa's ruby-red lipstick), along with a pastel softness in Rosé's opaque mesh and Lisa's Rodarte ruffled lace. There was also an overwhelming sense of mystery, sensuality and confidence in their expressions. It was a photo you could look at for ages. Naturally all five versions of the cover quickly sold out.

When asked on their US trip about any comeback plans, Blackpink had been unforthcoming, but on *Strahan and Sara* Jisoo had hinted that one might be on the way (and had seemed to want to say more). Blackpink finally finished the South-East Asia part of their world tour in the beginning of March and within a couple of weeks news was out that a new EP was on its way and that the girls were busy shooting the video.

When YG promised an altogether more intense release in terms of both music and choreography, the more cynical Blinks dismissed it as the usual marketing talk. Then the teaser posters came out. Lisa had shorter, ash-silver hair; Jennie (who had remained brown-haired throughout her entire career) looked sensational as a platinum blonde; Jisoo had a fiery crimson look; and Rosé, so often the delicate petal, was the only member to get a full-length shot, bossing it in layers of black leather with rose-gold hair tied tight in a ponytail. The following official group teaser poster looked like something from a movie or a Lara Croft-style game. The four members were badass female warriors, dressed in combat-like attire and standing among the rubble of a derelict doorway. They stared out at the camera like they meant serious business. Expectations had been well and truly stoked.

The *Kill This Love* EP was released on 5 April 2019 on the stroke of midnight after an hour-long V Live show. Two million viewers logged in to watch the girls discuss the new songs and be generally wonderful. They were now so much at ease in one another's company that they could tease each other (in the TMI section Jisoo even revealed how Lisa always tells her when she is going to the bathroom), help out when another member was flailing and talk excitedly about the new release.

There was plenty to be excited about, too, starting with the music video. A series of beautifully shot fantasy and nightmare scenarios, bordering on the surreal and punctuated by fierce and assertive choreography, it is a feast for the eyes. Scenes stay in the mind: Jennie luxuriant in the swan sunset; box-braided Lisa tearing up the crazy-coloured cereal supermarket; Jisoo in strange pink headgear and submerged up to her neck; tearful Rosé driving like her life depended on it (she couldn't actually drive, but the video was still banned by some Korean channels as she wasn't wearing a seat belt!); and the whole group dancing ferociously inside a giant bear trap.

If the video sacrifices plot for style, it really doesn't matter, because from start to finish it is an extravaganza of high fashion. As expected, the very latest catwalk collections from Chanel, Givenchy, Alexander McQueen and Versace are plundered for the girls' outfits. These make for some stand-out images, such as Jennie in the white Chanel La Pausa gown at the opening of the

In three short minutes, the video team, led by director Hyun Seung-seo, magnificently portrays the girls as both pretty and delicate, and as tough and streetwise.

video; Lisa's eye-catching oversized Givenchy crystal-encrusted glasses; the beautiful McQueen dress worn by a windswept Rosé; and archer Jisoo's metallic pleated silk Givenchy gown.

Lesser-known designer wear from around the world is also used widely to give the girls' elegance a rebellious edge. Items from edgy Seoul brand YCH often appear (Jennie's black and white lace bodysuit, for example), along with clothing from German futuristic label Me Dic Al (Rosé's space-cadet beige, grey and black crop jacket) and Danish unisex designer Heliot Emil (Jisoo's half-crop shirt).

In three short minutes, the video team, led by director Hyun Seung-seo, magnificently portrays the girls as both pretty and delicate, and as tough and streetwise. They channel Gwen Stefani, Ariana Grande, Harley Quinn from the *Batman* series and even Barbie. Make-up alternates between smoky tones and glittery pink, with diamante stick-ons added at will. Lisa's hair transformations may be the most obvious – clip-ons on her shorter cut enable her to play with blue and blonde looks and even grey cornrows – but the others change too. Rosé's champagne-gold locks take on the hairpins that Jennie made fashionable in 'Solo', tight side braids and a wild-child loose braid; while Jisoo's new crimson hair, in one of the video's prized beauty moments, is given the slicked-back wet-look treatment. Jennie went full Lara Croft in a look that would become iconic. Not only does she sport a long, braided ponytail, but she has the most amazing gradient smoky eyes, accentuated by crystals glued to their inner corner and set off with a lush pink lipstick.

And if all that wasn't enough, there was a song going on too! For those who had followed Blackpink's musical output, 'Kill This Love' was a logical progression. It had the insistent bass, the quirky hook (this time in the form of a horn-produced riff), the catchy onomatopoeic line and an EDM beat segueing into gentle piano-backed vocal sections or in-your-face rapping. It even included a return for the classic 'Blackpink in your area!' chant. For those – and there were still many – who hadn't encountered the group's sound before, it was a new and exciting dance track, rap number and earworm all in one. With a nod to their forthcoming US appearances, its generous English-language parts were more like a Japanese release than a Korean one.

The singing and rap parts give authority to the song's message of having the strength to end a toxic relationship and help impart an anthemic quality to 'Kill This Love'. There is a case to be made for each of the members' roles in sculpting the song. Rosé has the ability to convey emotion while delivering a strong and striking vocal, Jisoo has the measured, calming, just keeping-it-all-in lines, Jennie's growling vocals make the chorus, and Lisa snarls and bites as never before, but it is the sum of the parts that makes the song a classic.

'Kill This Love' was an instant hit, smashing records everywhere. The video amassed 56.7 million views in its first twenty-four hours, surpassing the 55.4 million YouTube record set by Ariana Grande's 'Thank U, Next' MV. Less than two days later it became the fastest video ever to reach 100 million views, this time beating Psy's 'Gangnam Style'. It reached the number one spot on iTunes in thirty-seven countries, including the US, where Blackpink became the first-ever Korean girl group (and the first all-female group since Destiny's Child) to top the charts. In the UK it reached number thirty-three, beating the group's own record ('Kiss and Make Up' made number thirty-six) for the highest-charting single in UK history by a female K-pop act.

While 'Kill This Love' was making pop headlines around the world, Blinks were busy discovering the delights of new Blackpink material in the three other new songs on the EP. 'Don't Know What to Do' was the second song from the EP that the group would promote and it was such a change – in style and attitude – from the title track. Bringing the pink side to the fore, the group project a far more conventional vulnerable feel in a bubbly and irresistible EDM bop that takes hold and never lets go. The vocals are exquisite (Rosé excelling in a central role) with a hands-in-the-air, singalong chorus (handily in English) that was bound to be a highlight of future live performances. It was an instant favourite among reviewers and some online commentators; some Blinks even preferred it to the lead single.

The inevitable audience response to the line 'Can I kick it?' on the next track must also have been on Teddy's mind when he wrote the much fiercer 'Kick It'. Another break-up celebration song, it rises and falls, held together by a strumming background acoustic guitar, resonating bass and the control of the vocals until it meets another classic Lisa rap or the infectious chorus. With such genre-jumping, Blinks listening for the first time must have wondered where the EP would go next. The answer was 'Hope Not', a tender heartfelt ballad backed by a simple soft electric guitar that could be filed next to 'Stay'. The EP was completed with a dubstep, club-friendly remix of 'Ddu-du Ddu-du'. *Kill This Love* had the same roaring success as the single, reaching the top ten in album charts around the world. The US reaction to the release was perhaps the most stunning: it placed at number one in the World Albums chart but, astoundingly, also reached number ten in the US Album chart.

Those anticipating the full choreography for 'Kill This Love' and 'Don't Know What to Do' didn't have long to wait. When the group appeared on *Show! Music Core* on 6 April Jennie was showing off her heavy, deep black bangs and straight hair, Lisa tossed her ash-coloured locks, Jisoo had that sophisticated side parting and Rosé looked great as a blonde. Their outfits were versions of black and claret warrior uniforms adorned by buckles and customized rollercoaster belts. In contrast, for 'Don't Know What to Do', they wore floral and check patterned dresses, appearing for all the world like innocent girls next door. Then, the next day, they took to the stage at *Inkigayo* in their full-on *Tomb Raider*-influenced outfits, complete with tight crop tops, leather garter straps and heavy boots, switching to a simple all-white outfit for 'Don't Know What to Do'. The black/pink, girl-crush/girl-group sides of the group had never been more distinct.

The 'Kill This Love' choreography, devised by Kiel Tutin and Kyle Hanagami (and, according to YG, two other world-class choreographers), was acclaimed by many as Blackpink's best yet. The girls dance as individuals, in pairs (Jennie with Jisoo, Rosé with Lisa) and as a foursome in a dynamic and hard-hitting sequence that includes the iconic salutes, shotgun move, heart-splitting action and Lisa kicking down the (imaginary) door. The dance-practice video was released just days after their comeback and was soon racking up views. Within two months it had been watched 100 million times.

Blackpink recorded their performance for the following week's

Inkigayo, but by that time they had already flown out to the USA for Coachella and their tour. It seemed telling that their priority was making headway in the US rather than increasing their popularity in South Korea, because now, more than anyone else in K-pop history, Blackpink was first and foremost an international group.

TWELVE

COACHELLA
HOW THE WEST WAS WON

A tent in the middle of the Colorado Desert in California might seem a strange place for a group used to playing the arenas and sports domes of Asia to make their US debut. But this was no ordinary tent and no ordinary desert. This was Coachella, the most prestigious music festival in the world, and Blackpink were about to introduce themselves to the USA.

Coachella had been established at the turn of the twenty-first century as an indie rock festival. Although it had kept its alternative feel, it had soon turned to other genres with legendary performances from Prince, Madonna, Kanye West, Lady Gaga, a reunited Dr Dre and Snoop Dogg, Daft Punk and, in 2018, Beyoncé, who had turned it into Beychella, putting the Indio Empire Polo Club venue firmly on the map. Every year, tens of thousands flocked to the sun-soaked venue for some of the biggest names in modern music.

Most of Coachella's stages have the beautiful desert landscape as a backdrop, but the Sahara tent where Blackpink would play on both Fridays of the festival's two weekends was the EDM house.

More like an aircraft hangar than any tent, it throbbed with lasers, lights and screens – and over 10,000 festival-goers ready to dance. 'I can't believe how many people came out tonight! Is this real?' exclaimed a rapt Rosé on stage. 'This has to be computer graphics.' The audience consisted of enough Blinks displaying their pink light sticks to make the group feel welcome and plenty of others already familiar with 'Kill This Love', but there were many new to K-pop who were there to be won over.

'Us coming all the way from South Korea, we didn't know what to expect, and obviously we – you guys and us – we're from totally different worlds,' she said, 'but tonight I think we've learned so deeply that music brings us [together] as one.'

From their powerful opening of 'Ddu-du Ddu-du' and 'Forever Young', Blackpink did just that in a blistering fifty-minute set into which they squeezed thirteen songs. They came to party. Dressed in festival-appropriate black, white and sparkly outfits enhanced by plenty of jewellery to catch the light and supported by a live band, The Band Six, who were willing to rock out, the girls gave it their all in their dance synchronicity, the raps, which were more savage than ever, and some genuinely eye-opening vocal moments. And they were having a good time. The UK music magazine *NME* noted, 'Their faces are an almost permanent display for broad, genuine grins, while, after "Whistle", Jisoo gives Jennie a tap on the elbow and a giggle that seem to say, "Can you believe this is happening?"'

The feel-good mood extended to the group's interactions with the audience as they chatted and initiated Mexican waves. Aussie

Rosé took the lead, especially in expressing what the event meant in terms of Blackpink, K-pop and the West. 'Us coming all the way from South Korea, we didn't know what to expect, and obviously we – you guys and us – we're from totally different worlds,' she said, 'but tonight I think we've learned so deeply that music brings us [together] as one.'

In the Sahara tent, in New York's Times Square, where the show had been streamed live on a huge screen, and among the press at Coachella, Blackpink had wowed so many with their charisma and talent. *Variety* wrote, 'It wasn't always easy to tell who in the audience was a hardcore fan and who was in the process of discovery, given that the enthusiasm levels often matched.' The *LA Times*' review of the festival featured a superb photo of Rosé mid-hair flick and renowned K-pop correspondent Jeff Benjamin perhaps captured it best, tweeting, 'Oh I'm obsessed. They transcended their past performances and looked like global superstars. I haven't said this about a lot of K-pop acts but they really brought it.'

Blackpink were still reeling from the success of their Coachella performance as they promoted 'Kill This Love' and the US tour in LA. In interviews they seemed genuinely shocked by the reaction they had received, describing it as bigger and better than they had ever imagined it could be. Jennie hailed the time on stage as the most intense hour of her life. 'There was too much energy,' she said, before adding, 'I'm still not over it.' Rosé went even further, calling it the best feeling she'd ever felt in twenty-two years of existence.

They might not have felt exactly the same about their appearance on James Corden's *The Late Late Show*, when they were persuaded to play the host's favourite game, Flinch. This involves the 'victims' standing behind a glass panel while an assortment of fruit is fired at them at great speed. Could they outsmart Corden by not flinching? It was quickly agreed that Jennie was the most easily shocked of the four (something Blinks already knew all too well), so cruelly she was picked to be the first target, with Jisoo directed to stand beside her. James Corden caught Jennie by surprise, firing mid-conversation, and the poor girl jumped out of her skin. Despite also being in the firing line, Jisoo was as cool as you like and proved to be the most unflappable of them all, as both Lisa and Rosé couldn't prevent themselves from recoiling.

However, we know these girls can be badass, too, when the occasion calls for it and they turned the tables on James, placing him behind the screen. Cleverly they lined up so he couldn't see who held the firing button and they secured the flinch to get even with their host. Appropriately, it transpired it was Jennie who had pressed the button. That night Corden tweeted, 'I'm a Blink. Deal with it' and he turned his Twitter account into a Blackpink fan account with pics and gifs of the girls on the show, as well as the legendary tweet: 'Lisa & Rosé protecting each other during Flinch is friendship goals.'

Before they returned to Coachella, they had another major engagement: their first North American headline show, at the Los Angeles Forum. The sea of light sticks turning the 15,000-strong crowd into a pink ocean was the perfect welcome and a sign of how far they had already progressed in America. In return, they treated the screaming fan girls and boys to the hits (even 'Kiss and Make Up' without Dua Lipa), the latest songs from the EP and the solo performances in a scintillating 100-minute show. They seemed truly amazed to find an American audience singing back to them in Korean on 'Don't Know What to Do' and left the stage on a real high, with Jennie promising, 'This is just the beginning, so watch out for us.' It certainly seemed like former One Direction member Harry Styles, who sat transfixed in the VIP section of the audience, would be doing just that.

The group returned to Coachella to do it all over again a week later. The word was now officially out, not just among music fans but with the biggest stars in the industry. The girls were not only winning new followers but making friends, too. Whether it was bopping with Khalid, hanging out with Jaden Smith or having pics taken with Diplo, Blackpink had arrived and were having a ball. Lisa was filmed dancing with Willow Smith at Kanye West's Sunday Service dance party and Jennie, Rosé and Lisa watched Billie Eilish's set (Jennie later shared a photo of her hugging the singer with the caption 'My crush').

Most attention came from the members' link-up with festival headliner Ariana Grande. The '7 Rings' singer had mentioned she intended to catch Blackpink's Coachella set in a tweet that went viral a couple of weeks before the festival and when she spotted them in the crowd at her performance she invited the girls backstage to share a photo (Jisoo missed out as she was resting at the time). The following day, like true fan girls, they were seen showing off the dust masks they had been given from her brand-new NASA merchandise collection. The excited Blinks clamoured for a collaboration following the (albeit brief) online friendship.

Coachella had given the members a massive confidence boost. They had played alongside top Western artists and had proved to be their equals (some claiming they had even surpassed them), and they now embarked on the rest of their North American tour, winding their way up to Chicago, Ontario in Canada, and then down to New Jersey, Georgia and Texas. Each of the sell-out dates was a whirlwind of excitement. Fabulous lasers filled the air with neon-pink spotlights while fireworks, confetti and pyrotechnic effects had the audience open-mouthed. Giant LED screens provided a visually dazzling, ever-changing background, The Band Six's rocking instrumentals kept the audience on their feet between costume changes and the hyped-up Blinks held excitement levels at their peak by participating in chants, singalongs and light-stick waving. The members' gratitude and love for their fans was evident in every city as they smiled, joked and waved their way across the States.

Blinks were frequently reduced to tears of happiness, but the emotion of the evening could also get to the band members. In Hamilton, Ontario, Rosé teared up during her piano-accompanied solo and felt the need to explain to the audience, saying, 'I made such a fool of myself. It only happens when I am in the moment. You guys made me feel so comfortable.' Lisa was reduced to tears, too. When waving at the crowd, she noticed someone telling a blind member of the audience what was happening. When he waved back it was too much for Lisa. Jennie immediately noticed and gave her a hug – that's what friends are for!

It was those attending the Newark concert on 1 May who got the biggest surprise of the tour, though. 'A friend of mine told me Blackpink will perform in Newark and that we should

> Rosé teared up during her piano-accompanied solo and felt the need to explain to the audience, saying, 'I made such a fool of myself. It only happens when I am in the moment. You guys made me feel so comfortable.'

go. I was like, wait, maybe I should get up and do "Kiss and Make Up" with them,' explained their friend and collaborator Dua Lipa. The backstage meet-up, which appeared in the *Blackpink Diaries* fly-on-the-wall series about the tour, showed the group so excited to meet their collaborator. The feeling was mutual, with Dua Lipa declaring, 'Oh my god, you guys are stunning!' When they introduced her on stage, the Blinks' reaction was just as enthusiastic and after Dua Lipa had slotted in perfectly like a fifth member of the group, everyone took a second to take in what had happened. Rosé screamed, 'That was crazy!' while all the clearly emotional Jennie could muster was, 'Oh my God, we're so, like, star-struck right now.'

What a month it had been! Blackpink flew back to South Korea after their final American concert in Duluth, Texas, having made so many friends and new fans. Those early plans of YG to create a group that would appeal to a global audience and not just a small band of K-pop fans in each country was bearing fruit. Blinks loved Jisoo, Jennie, Rosé and Lisa for who and what they were, but thousands of others also understood their image, got the concept and loved the dance and vocals. The girls themselves had little time to dwell on all this, though, because in just a week they were off to conquer a new continent – Europe.

Their European tour began in Amsterdam and moved on to England, where they played the Manchester Arena on the eve of the second anniversary of the tragic bombing that had taken place after an Ariana Grande concert at the venue. The group were incredibly sensitive to the situation. They opened with a message of support to the friends and families of those who had suffered, which ended with #OneLoveManchester. They also changed elements of their performance, including dropping 'Ddu-Du

Ddu-Du', their usual opening song (they played the remix, which doesn't have the gun actions in the encore), and amending 'Whistle' lyrics and 'Kill This Love' choreography. At the encore stage, in an emotional introduction, they dedicated 'Stay' to the victims, which gave the usual crowd singalong even more poignancy than usual. It was a challenging evening on which to play that venue, but all four managed to display respect and sensitivity, while still enabling their fans to enjoy a thrilling show.

> Live K-pop acts don't tend to visit Australia very often, so Blinks there gave the warmest of welcomes to Blackpink.

While less emotional, the rest of the European tour – which took in London, Berlin, Paris and Barcelona – was a sell-out success. Perfect in performance (apart from the London show, where a faulty lift briefly left Jennie stuck under the stage!) and spontaneous and charming when addressing the audience, the group found fans cheering wildly and singing as enthusiastically as Blinks back in Asia.

After a single concert in Macau on 8 June, while the other three returned home, Rosé wrote on her Instagram account, 'Guess where I'm going?' She was returning to her family home to enjoy a precious few days with her family and friends before Blackpink played their first-ever concerts in Australia. Live K-pop acts don't tend to visit Australia very often, so Blinks there gave the warmest of welcomes to Blackpink. They were thrilled to have their very own Aussie K-pop star and Rosé revelled in being home, engaging the crowd with her memories of growing up there and celebrating with them. It was certainly the first Blackpink concert at which 'Aussie Aussie Aussie, Oi Oi Oi', the cry usually heard at sports venues, rang out, but Rosé joined in from the stage and even managed to persuade Lisa to chant as well!

The world tour finally came to an end in Bangkok, where it had begun. By then, home-town girl Lisa's new solo 'Swalla' dance had gone viral, so it was only fitting that she again earned the plaudits with her updated choreography to the track. For the four giving their all on stage it had been an exhausting six months on the road (interrupted only by a blistering comeback and a triumphant Coachella), but each stop had been a victory. Blinks had greeted them enthusiastically in each new town and city; they had cheered, sung and chanted through every second of the concerts and had shown each of the members such love. Blackpink weren't just in your area – they were now, officially, everywhere.

JISOO: MISS KOREA

Real name: Kim Ji-soo

Stage name: Jisoo

Nicknames: Chuu, Chichu, MC Chu, Fake Maknae, Miss Korea

Nationality: South Korean

Born: Gunpo, South Korea

Date of birth: 3 January 1995

Height: 162 cm

Zodiac sign: Capricorn

Chinese zodiac sign: Dog

Siblings: two (older brother and older sister)

Position: lead vocalist, visual

Trainee period: five years

Instagram: @sooyaaa__

For YG Entertainment, Jisoo was the revolution. A company that had built a reputation on idols who were supremely talented, rather than supremely beautiful, chose Jisoo, an obvious 'visual' (the K-pop term for a stand-out beauty). From the outset, Jisoo was labelled 'The YG Idol with the SM Face'. She had the classic Korean looks that SM Entertainment traditionally valued and yet here she was debuting for the 'cool' YG. If proof was needed, Jisoo was even scouted by SM at a YG concert, although fortunately for YG they had already signed her up as a trainee!

Jisoo grew up in a small city just fifteen miles (twenty-five kilometres) south of Seoul. She is the youngest of three children in a fairly affluent family and remains close to her sister, Kim Ji-yoon, and brother, Kim Jung-hun; her brother's wedding in May 2019 was attended by all four members of Blackpink. As a child Jisoo received plenty of attention, especially when she was singing and dancing, and this love of performing led her to audition for YG Entertainment in 2011, when she was just sixteen.

Her school friends' testimonies and early photos have confirmed that Jisoo was extremely pretty even as a young teenager. The picture Blinks particularly cherish is one of her in her school uniform sporting a shoulder-length, thick black bob hairstyle with long straight bangs. At a fansign event in 2019, one fan enlarged the picture to actual size and cut out the face, and all the Blackpink members had great fun posing with their pre-debut Jisoo hair!

Jisoo didn't just audition on the basis of her looks, though. She had a good singing voice as well, and took on Lee Eun-mi's 1989 hit 'I Have a Lover'– the only Blackpink member to choose a ballad at their audition. She has since revealed that the response wasn't exactly encouraging, as she was told, 'At least you're singing in key.' She was asked about the ring on her finger, to check she wasn't dating, and was also asked who her favourite act was. She chose the SM boy group TVXQ, which the YG boss would remember – for the next few years, whenever he saw her, he would call her the TVXQ fan.

The company were obviously convinced of her beauty and charisma and felt her singing had potential, and in July 2011 Jisoo became a YG Entertainment trainee. Jennie and Lisa were already there and Jisoo soon made strong friendships with them, as well as the other potential members of the planned group. Training was tough, especially for someone without a strong vocal or dance background, but Jisoo worked hard, often sleeping for only three or four hours a night.

> Training was tough, especially for someone without a strong vocal or dance background, but Jisoo worked hard, often sleeping for only three or four hours a night.

Jisoo would spend five years as trainee, but she had good reason to believe she could succeed. Cast in various adverts for school uniforms, cameras, video games and smartphones, she received some recognition, and her appearances in videos for Epik High's 'Spoiler' and Hi Suhyun's 'I'm Different' in 2014 raised some eyebrows. She even had a cameo, among more famous Korean celebrities, in a TV K-Drama called *Producer*. However, it was when she appeared opposite the incredibly popular actor Lee Min-ho in a 2015 commercial for Samsonite Red suitcases that many began to notice the gorgeous young girl.

They would soon find out much more. Back in January 2013, Jisoo had been revealed as a member of YG's new girl group, but finally in June 2016, three and a half years later, she became the third and eldest Blackpink member to be confirmed to the public. Her teaser photos portrayed her as a cute schoolgirl, a rock chick and an alluring temptress – there was no doubt she had the looks, but could she sing and dance? After the Blackpink debut the jury was out. Her singing was restricted to backing vocals and, compared to the others, her dancing lacked confidence. She was not the 'dance hole' as some harsher critics cruelly labelled her, but her moves needed improvement.

> Jisoo did a great job of raising the profile of Blackpink and of proving she was indeed a superstar. Those who questioned her dancing capabilities were proved wrong in her performances on the show.

Meanwhile, another side of Jisoo was emerging. In interviews she was forthcoming when the others were shy; she was engaging, funny and confident when speaking to presenters. It therefore surprised no one when, in February 2017, she was announced as a permanent presenter on the music show *Inkigayo*. Jisoo took her place as a host alongside NCT's Doyoung and GOT7's Jinyoung, and the three of them struck up an immediate chemistry. JinJiDo, as they became known, were one of the most popular presenting teams the show had ever had.

Jisoo did a great job of raising the profile of Blackpink and of proving she was indeed a superstar. Those who questioned her dancing capabilities were proved wrong in her performances on the show, especially in the special stage when she danced to Ariana Grande's 'Side to Side' and in the 'Uptown Funk' performance with Jinyoung. MC Chu, as she was fondly nicknamed (which, in turn, she wittily contorted to M-Shih Tzu), interacted with other artists,

Jisoo

Jennie

Rosé

Lisa

Jisoo

Jennie

Rosé

Lisa

smiled constantly and was full of energy. Her stint on *Inkigayo* lasted a year, but by that time she was ensconced in the hearts of many of the Korean public.

Jisoo was also established as one of K-pop's 4D stars. The term 4D is widely used in Korean pop culture, applied to any character who is a little odd, different or slightly weird – and it is intended as a compliment. Jisoo earned her 4D reputation through her quirky actions in interviews and filming – performing sudden dance moves, pulling faces or just being random, but always in the cutest way. Blinks love her over-enthusiasm for chicken on *Weekly Idol* or her flu-jab discussion with Rosé on *Blackpink House*, where she ends the conversation by saying 'I like flu'! Perhaps the most memorable incident was at the 2017 Seoul Music Festival, when the camera briefly showed the celebrity-audience section. There, as members of girl group Red Velvet demurely watched the performance, Jisoo attracted attention as she tried to balance a water bottle on her shoulder.

Equally 4D and just as beguiling are Jisoo's made-up words and songs. Early in Blackpink's life she came up with 'nyongan' – the word *annyeong* (hello) mixed up – for hello or goodbye and 'ppoong', a word even Jisoo admits has no meaning, which has the advantage that you can say it whenever you want! In *Blackpink House*, you never had to wait long for a snippet of Jisoo's self-composed ditties, including 'If it's cold, you'll catch a cold', 'The ants are working hard' and a host of songs celebrating food, from radishes to chicken skewers.

Jisoo is clearly the mood-maker of the group, but she is also the name-maker. As the eldest member, she bestowed the name Jendeukie on Jennie (because Jennie was so clingy when they shared a room), while she had fun playing on Lisa's name, coming up with Nallalisa (Korean for 'Flying Lisa') or Jolisa (Korean for 'chef') when Lisa cooks. Finally, when Rosé was given her stage name, Jisoo kept coming to her door saying 'Pasta, Pasta'. She seems to have a close and easy-going relationship with all the members. Jisoo and Jennie had known each other for only three days when they went to a Korean public bath together and shared their dreams and aspirations in the steam room. They became roommates and have an enduring friendship, referred to by Blinks as 'Jensoo'.

Meanwhile, Jisoo and Lisa – nicknamed 'Lisoo' – are the crazy twins. There's always something extra going on when the 'fake *maknae*' (youngest in the group) and the real *maknae* are together – a tweet of them both doing an impromptu hand dance went viral in 2017 and received over a million views. Jisoo's rapport with Rosé might not seem so intense, but their appearances together on V Live broadcasts and photoshoots for Kiss Me and Moonshot cosmetics show that seven years together has brought them as close as sisters.

Someone as outgoing as Jisoo obviously has many friends outside Blackpink as well. Fans especially like to see her with Nayeon from Twice (who was a trainee with them at YG) and Red Velvet's Seulgi, who struck up a friendship with her when they appeared together on the web drama *Idol Drama Operation Team*. She can also number two upcoming models and actresses in Hong Soo-joo and Yu Hye-won among her close friends. But Jisoo's best friend of all is male – her beautiful white Maltese dog Dalgom. Born on 5 May 2015, Dalgom has been by Jisoo's side ever since. Shy and fond of sleeping, Dalgomie (as Jisoo calls him) is so docile. Only Lisa manages to rile him up, and her constant teasing has made an enemy of the cute-as-anything pooch!

At the same time as Jisoo's personality was endearing her to Blinks around the world, her other talents were attracting attention, too. The harsh criticisms of her dancing disappeared as she turned in killer performances time after time. Had she been working on her dancing or was it just a matter of her growing confidence? Whatever the answer, Jisoo was no longer the weak link in the Blackpink dance line-up; she was fluid and on point.

Jisoo's vocals were also being recognized as a key element of the group's songs. Although she still wasn't getting enough lines to really show off her voice, Blinks were picking up on her massive contribution to the 'hidden' vocals and the way she anchored the vocal track and contributed masterful harmonizing. Listening to Blackpink 'MR Removed' songs, where the instrumental track is muted as much as possible, her voice is distinctive and seriously good. Many now credit Jisoo with having the most stable voice of all the members and some Blinks call her the 'hidden backbone of Blackpink'.

In the live solo stages she finally got a chance to display her vocal talents. Performing 'Clarity', originally by Zedd but with Korean lyrics Jisoo had written by herself, her voice was powerful and she reached the high notes with ease. Even Zedd himself tweeted his approval. Another favourite is her duet with Rosé on the TV show *Radio Star*, where the duo sang an acoustic cover of Justin Bieber's 'Love Yourself'. Here, she not only harmonized beautifully but also showed she could sing perfectly well in English.

No one ever had any doubts about Jisoo's optical appeal, though. Blackpink stylist Choi Kyoung-won has described Jisoo's style as 'elegant with girlish appeal' and the group's visual has always carried it off effortlessly. From the blue Lucky Chouette dress of 'Whistle' to the Givenchy metallic lamé dress in 'Kill This

Love', and the simple but gorgeous black and pink outfit she wore on her *Inkigayo* MC debut to the red velvet crop top and choker combination at the 2018 MMAs, she has worn many iconic outfits. Her hair, too, has made waves, especially the purple of the 'As If It's Your Last' comeback, the red of 'Kill This Love' and, of course, the amazing pink bob wig in the 'Ddu-du Ddu-du' music video.

Off-duty Jisoo often rocks a cuter and more effervescent look, wearing a lot of white with vibrant or pastel colours. Her style is more feminine than the other members' – she likes flouncy, printed textiles and elegant shirt dresses with a belt or plain single-coloured skater skirts matched with a brighter patterned top. She'll be seen in a boyish graphic T-shirt and ripped jeans, but she'll still invariably have a cute beanie or choker and her hair down to give it a girly edge. Fortunately, Blinks can always check out her outfits on her Instagram account as she posts a constant stream of beautiful selfies (often called *selcas* in Korea) and photos taken by Lisa.

> Jisoo's global popularity is clear from her 18 million followers on Instagram.

In a group with an international outlook and English-speaking members, Jisoo, born and raised in South Korea, was always one for the home fans. She soon picked up the nickname Miss Korea and remains popular in her native land (only Jennie in the group ranks above her in polls, with Jisoo featuring among the top ten idols in South Korea). Although her popularity is highest in Asia (she speaks excellent Japanese and Chinese), Jisoo's global popularity is clear from her 18 million followers on Instagram. In June 2019, although she appeared for just eleven seconds in the TV drama *Arthdal Chronicles*, #JisooOnArthdalChronicles went to number one on Twitter's worldwide trends in twelve countries, not only in Asia but also in the UK, Italy, Brazil and Saudi Arabia.

As the eldest member of a group with no leader, Jisoo has often stepped up to the role. The other members have said that they've seen her cry only once (when Jennie injured her ankle rehearsing for their debut on *Inkigayo*), although she has admitted she sometimes cries in secret as she feels the need to be strong for the others. However, during interviews on the tour to North America and the UK, Jisoo took a back seat and was often silent or only spoke briefly. Many assumed her English was poor, but it had more to do with allowing the more fluent speakers to take the lead. Jisoo's understanding of English is, in fact, excellent, and her speaking is improving all the time.

Could YG have guessed an idol supposedly selected for her looks would turn out to be just as talented as any of their other stars? Was this what YG planned all along? Certainly, in the few years since Blackpink's debut, Jisoo has been a leader, a friend, a flawless performer and an entertainer, and has proved she is so much more than just an extraordinary visual.

JENNIE: THE SECRET WEAPON

Real name: Jennie Kim

Stage name: Jennie

Nicknames: Jendeukie, NiNi, Human Gucci

Nationality: South Korean

Born: Anyang, South Korea

Date of birth: 16 January 1996

Height: 163 cm

Zodiac sign: Capricorn

Chinese zodiac sign: Pig

Siblings: none

Position: main rapper, vocalist

Trainee period: five years, eleven months

Instagram: @jennierubyjane and @lesyeuxdenini

Back in 2013, three years before Blackpink's debut, the buzz at YG Entertainment was that they had a 'secret weapon' in training. Jennie was then a third-year trainee and it was clear that great things were expected of her, but that was hardly surprising. YG had signed a natural beauty who spoke fluent English and Korean and could rap like a senior. As their plans for a new girl group called Pink Punk developed, their secret weapon Jennie was the first name on the list.

Perhaps Jennie's parents had a hunch their baby would be a K-pop star when she was born in a satellite city of Seoul in January 1996. Unusually for South Korea, she was given a Western name, so there would be no need for her to take a stage name years later. Even more helpful for a future *hallyu* singer, her parents sent their only child to live in Auckland, New Zealand, when she was just ten years old. Jennie remembers being on a family holiday there when her mother asked if she liked it and if she would like to move there. Soon she found herself living with a homestay family and attending school in New Zealand. She would not return to live in South Korea for five years.

> Perhaps Jennie's parents had a hunch their baby would be a K-pop star when she was born in a satellite city of Seoul in January 1996; unusually for South Korea, she was given a Western name.

Her parents' plan was for Jennie to travel to the US and become a lawyer or teacher, but in a tearful and impassioned phone call from Auckland she persuaded them to support her dream of a career in music and let her return to Seoul. There she attended Chungdam, the 'idols' high school', in Gangnam. Jennie understood K-pop and knew exactly which company she wanted to join, singing and dancing to Rihanna's 'Take a Bow' at YG's summer audition in 2010. By August that year they were welcoming her as a trainee.

Jennie hadn't considered herself a rapper but, perhaps because of her fluency in English, YG set about turning her into one. In August 2012 they posted a clip of their sixteen-year-old star, dressed in black and white, with a hip-hop beanie and her hair falling over one eye, freestyle rapping to B.o.B's 'Strange Clouds'. It made a splash, with K-pop sites asking if this was the new CL (2NE1's rapper). Over the next year she would appear opposite G-Dragon in his music video for 'That XX', and feature on Li Hi's song 'Special' and Seungri's 'GG Be'. YG also posted a sixty-second clip of her covering Wale's 'Lotus Flower Bomb'. Next came her biggest break yet, as the featured artist on G-Dragon's single 'Black', and she appeared alongside him on TV music show *Inkigayo* wearing a simple black dress and with a blonde underside to her black hair. Suddenly the words 'YG Princess' were being bandied about.

However, it would be another three years before Jennie was revealed as 'New Girl Group – Member #1'. She seemed to find those trainee days particularly tough, especially the stressful monthly tests in choreography, singing and styling. She dedicated herself to improving her rapping, looking to Lauryn Hill, TLC and, of course, Rihanna for inspiration, and she claims to have written over a hundred songs during this time. The postponement of each promised debut date was heart-breaking, but served only to make her and the other girls work harder and harder. Now Jennie admits that this harsh period was ultimately what made Blackpink the tough, close-knit outfit they are today.

When they were finally set to debut, the teaser pics of Jennie confirmed what K-pop aficionados had already gleaned. She looked sensational and could carry off both an innocent look in a school uniform or a wild-child vibe in AC/DC rock T-shirt and tight silver trousers. And her performances were equally impressive. Her rapping was skilful and she could deliver rapid and powerful lines, as well as mellow and soulful ones, while remaining full of swag, plus her dancing was bewitching and full of energy. This princess was the real deal.

As Jennie appeared on more broadcasts and reality shows, it became apparent that the 'badass' rapper was actually a cute pussy cat. She was sweet and lively, and cared deeply about the other members. It was, however, her appearances on the variety show *Running Man* that led to claims that she had 'stolen the nation's heart'. The long-running TV series gave celebrities games and tasks to complete, and Jennie threw herself into every challenge. The episode where viewers really fell in love with her was when she teamed up with regular cast member and resident coward Lee Kwang-soo to enter a haunted house. A confident Jennie took the lead, but gradually became more and more spooked by the experience, until she was yelling, screaming and crying. She was cast as unlucky and easily scared, but cute and funny, and incidents like sharing a giant T-shirt with the ungainly tall Kwang-soo, wearing shark onesie pyjamas and running away from a butterfly all added to her growing popularity.

It wasn't long before Jennie's two furry companions were receiving all the love, too. Kai, a white Cocker Spaniel with doleful eyes, wasn't seen too much as he lived with Jennie's parents and was already five years old when Blackpink debuted, but Kuma, named after the popular Japanese mascot Kumamon, and also known as Kuku, was just a puppy. The brown Pomeranian (who likes sweet potatoes!) became a star of many V Live broadcasts, including one famous episode named 'Kumayah', where Lisa got the cute little pup to 'dance' to 'Boombayah'.

V Live programmes, *Blackpink House* and other clips have revealed Jennie to be a caring, sensitive woman who is close not only to all three Blackpink members but also to other K-pop stars, especially Nayeon from Twice, Irene of Red Velvet and Chahee from Melody Day. She is fun, unafraid to laugh at herself and occasionally can be pretty savage. Fans love to see her teaming up with Lisa, as the two are never far away from a giggling fit. The behind-the-scenes clip of their photoshoot together for *Cosmopolitan Korea* magazine is a classic example, as they go through six takes, each time breaking down in hysterics. The other side of Jennie is seen clearly in a show called *We Will Channel You*, where Jennie's tears well up when, for the first time, she sees how the members supported her when she went on TV to promote her 'Solo' release.

From Blackpink's first appearances Jennie was recognized as a fashionista. The group's stylist, Choi Kyung-won, called her appeal 'cute but sexy' and the sense of feminine mystique is ever-present in her appearances on stage and in the MVs. 'On stage, I like to portray my different sides as much as possible,' she told *Billboard* in 2017. 'I want to try a feminine style, but mix it up with sexy or hip-hop elements. When I pay attention to the little details, such as

The brown Pomeranian (who likes sweet potatoes!) became a star of many V Live broadcasts, including one famous episode named 'Kumayah', where Lisa got the cute little pup to 'dance' to 'Boombayah'.

matching accessories to the entire outfit, I only get more confident on stage.' What was perhaps most impressive was that she could rock nearly every kind of outfit: from ultra-sexy skin-tight black leather in the 'Ddu-du Ddu-du' video to the super-comfy Chanel pink and green striped sweater of 'Stay' to the highest of high-end style in the sophisticated and elegant $2,000 Balmain dress she wore to the 2018 Golden Disc Awards.

Jennie has earned the tag 'Human Gucci' for her designer stage outfits (she knows fans call her this but says she is 'embarrassed to say the nickname myself'). However, it was Chanel that picked up on her appeal by making her their Korean ambassador in 2018. They gave Jennie not only a whole new Chanel wardrobe but also a front-row seat at their Paris Fashion Week show. Wearing a fabulous Chanel white tweed belted minidress, she took her place next to Pharrell Williams and Pamela Anderson.

It isn't just her working clothes that have established Jennie's fashion-queen reputation. Whenever she is seen out and about, she just looks so chic, even in white crop tops, boyfriend jeans, statement T-shirts, athleisure wear and boots or sneakers. She might add a simple pendant, wear oversize glasses or shades and carry a designer bag, but she has an innate sense of style that is enhanced by her charisma and her delicate features, which can carry off a just-out-of-bed look as well as an exquisite make-up job.

With over 21 million followers on Instagram (she was awarded the Most Loved award by Korea Instagram in 2018), Jennie is not just fashion-conscious – she is also a serial trendsetter. She has generated interest in high-fashion items such as Marine Serre's crescent-moon-printed clothes and Chanel tweeds, but also in accessories, including the Gucci brooch, hair pins (which were later sold as 'Jennie pins') and even wearing a pink scrunchie as a bracelet.

Not one for dramatic changes in hair colour (the blonde teaser for 'Kill This Love' turned out to be a wig), Jennie is known for her 'fifty shades of brown'. Her make-up in the videos ranges from the outrageous to the subtle but across her Instagram selfies a sultry glamour puss emerges, with a love of smoky eyeshadow and peachy tones, cat eyes and red, red lips. Again, she has the ability to create trends, with bejewelled inner eyes and white eyeliner among the looks that have been picked up by stylists and fans. In 2019, Jennie's place as one of the faces of K-pop was confirmed when she was selected as the new face of K-beauty brand HERA. After she advertised their Red Vibe lip series, the sales increased five-fold and they were commonly known as 'Jennie's lipsticks'.

All of this came together when Jennie was selected to be the first member of Blackpink to have a solo release. The aptly named 'Solo' displayed the confidence she had developed as a singer, rapper and dancer, as well as the charisma and style she had developed in Blackpink. She admitted it was daunting to be the first of the group to go public with a solo project, but was amazed at the global success the single achieved. She would become the first-ever female solo K-pop artist to exceed 300 million views on YouTube.

The 'Solo' MV was like Jennie's modelling showreel. She paraded in sumptuous and distinctive locations in over twenty outfits, looking stunning in each and every one of them. In just under three minutes she goes from fragile girl to elegant princess to girl-crush rebel – with some considerable help from the likes of Burberry (the colourful cashmere motif jumper), Marine Serre (the silk ballgown), Chanel (the black swimsuit), Gucci (the crystal-embellished biker jacket), Paco Rabanne (the metal-mesh minidress) and enough others to have racked up a costume bill of over $50,000.

On her TV and other live performances, Jennie has proved she is more than just a pretty face or a clothes horse. For her solo performance at the 2018 SBS TV spectacular *Gayo Daejun*, she wore just one outfit (OK, it was a gorgeous black Balmain number) along with her famous hair pins, but in the midst of a troupe of dancers she took the focus and completely owned the stage. She brought power, energy and grace to the choreography and, at the end, without missing a beat, joined her fellow members as if she had never been apart from them. She would repeat this awesome performance in future Blackpink shows, including at Coachella, where she made *Billboard* magazine's 'Ten best things we saw at Coachella' list with a stage they described as 'mind-blowing'.

> The 'Solo' MV was like Jennie's modelling showreel. She paraded in sumptuous and distinctive locations in over twenty outfits, looking stunning in each and every one of them.

The US and European leg of the In Your Area tour came at a good time for Jennie. From the debut through to her solo single, her life had been on an upward trajectory. However, the mutual ending of her relationship with Kai from EXO, after it had been revealed by a Korean news outlet, could not have been easy for the young star. Also potentially distressing was a small but vociferous number of people who were critical of some of her recent performances (a 'lazy Jennie' video clip even went viral) and perceived favouritism towards her at the company. Fortunately, the USA in particular was a personal success for Jennie. With the Coachella love, a solo hit and as one of the two fluent English speakers of the group, she played a bigger role in interviews. She came away with an enhanced reputation and new celebrity friends, including Harry Styles, Ariana Grande and Billie Eilish.

Jennie's popularity is now greater than ever. On 8 August 2019 she launched a second Instagram account to celebrate Blackpink's third anniversary. Named @lesyeuxdenini ('the eyes of Nini' in French), it is a personal photography account of her life from May 2019 that bears the subtitle 'A story that eye witnessed'. It includes photos of her bandmates, her dogs, selfies and street scenes and in a matter of weeks accumulated nearly a million followers.

Jennie Kim has played a crucial role in Blackpink's success. She now ranks in the top fifty social-media influencers in the world (comparable with Lady Gaga) and her global popularity is evident from the continent-spanning list of the top five countries where her Instagram followers live: Indonesia, Brazil, USA, South Korea and the Philippines. Despite her solo success, Jendeukie is clearly still part of the close-knit group with whom she has spent nearly ten years and is beloved by millions of Blinks for her looks, talents, fashion sense and loveable personality. YG Entertainment certainly has deployed its 'secret weapon' to maximum effect.

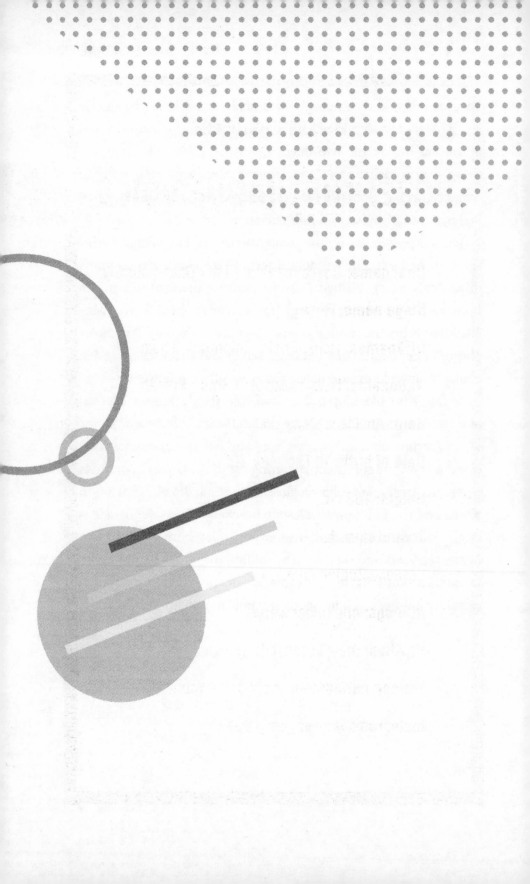

ROSÉ: THE UNIQUE VOICE

Real name: Roseanne Park / Park Chae-young

Stage name: Rosé

Nicknames: Rose, Rosie, Chipmunk, Pasta

Nationality: New Zealander / South Korean

Born: Auckland, New Zealand

Date of birth: 11 February 1997

Height: 168 cm

Zodiac sign: Aquarius

Chinese Zodiac sign: Ox

Siblings: one (older sister)

Position: main vocalist, lead dancer

Trainee period: four years, three months

Instagram: @roses_are_rosie

Back in 2017, in an interview with the *Sydney Morning Herald*, Rosé said, 'I'm just dreaming that one day I'll be able to come back to my home town and perform for everyone.' It might have seemed far-fetched back then, but in June 2019 her dream came true as their world tour took Blackpink to Australia, to both Sydney and Melbourne, the city she had left to begin her journey to stardom.

Although she was born in Auckland, New Zealand, Rosé's family moved to Box Hill, a suburb of Melbourne in Australia, when she was seven years old. She grew up a true Aussie, but both her parents are Korean and she was well aware of her Korean roots, attending a Korean Christian church where she sang and danced. Rosé enjoyed her studies at school and when Blackpink came to the city she delighted in returning there, even presenting a signed album to her favourite Japanese teacher. Just like her older sister, Alice, who went on to study law at university, Rosé might well have achieved academic success if destiny had not intervened.

In her second year of middle school, Rosé saved her money in order to buy a guitar. She found it difficult to learn to play, but – and this is a recurring theme – she gritted her teeth and persevered. She played the piano, too, and music soon became her obsession. Her father noticed her talent and encouraged her to travel to Sydney to attend the 2012 YG Entertainment audition. Modestly, she would say, he wanted her to go because she was obsessed with singing Beyoncé's 'Listen' at the time, but kept murdering the high notes. She joked, 'I think he was sick of me screaming at the top of my lungs on my piano, every night at like 12 a.m.'

Out of 400 hopefuls at the Sydney audition, it was Rosé who was invited by YG Entertainment to take up a place as a trainee in Seoul. She was just fifteen and setting off to live in a country she had seldom visited before. She arrived on 7 May 2012, the last of the members to join the company. That day is marked by Blinks as Chaelisa Day, when Lisa met the new recruit in the elevator. 'She was wearing a light-blue fitted shirt, skinny jeans, shoes like Vans and had a guitar,' Lisa recalled. 'I was like "Amazing, a foreigner! Amazing, she came from Australia!"' It wasn't long before she met her other future bandmates, citing an all-night singalong as their great bonding session. 'We just clicked,' Rosé said.

Rosé spent the least time of all the Blackpink members as a trainee, but they were years that severely tested the strength of her ambition and resolve.

Out of 400 hopefuls at the Sydney audition, it was Rosé who was invited by YG Entertainment to take up a place as a trainee in Seoul. She was just fifteen and setting off to live in a country she had seldom visited before.

Like the other girls, Rosé found trainee life tough. She'd call her parents in tears and her mother suggested she came home, but those teeth were gritted again. Inspired by Korean solo singer Gummy and US singer-songwriter Tori Kelly, Rosé redoubled her efforts. She must have been encouraged when, after just six months at the company, she featured on 'Without You', a track on an EP by G-Dragon. She was credited as '? from YG New Girl Group', and YG's biggest star raved about the young singer, becoming the first to call her voice unique.

It took nearly four years for the mystery singer to be named as Rosé, the stage name given to the girl known to her friends as Chae-young (which they continued to call her). She was the last of the four members of Blackpink to be revealed. Her debut teaser pictures showed off her piercing eyes, delicate features and long legs, with her hair changing from fiery red to black to light brown before they had even debuted. Amazingly for a debut group whose incredible beauty was the major talking point, Rosé's voice was identified by a large number of new Blackpink fans as strong, sweet and distinctive. Rosé herself was taken aback, as she hadn't realized her voice was that special and felt comforted by the fans' response to her vocals.

Rosé's first forays into the TV variety-show world presented her as a shy girl who preferred to remain silent wherever possible, bringing out her party pieces of 'a voice in a box' or rotating her wrist 360 degrees when forced. By 2017, however, she had grown in confidence enough to put herself forward without the group. She took part in *King of Masked Singer*, a show where idols perform in disguise. Rosé went under the mystery name of Circus Girl, wearing a mask that resembled a circus tent. She won her way through the first round with a powerful rendition of 'Livin' la Vida Loca' and returned the next week to sing Jung Seung-hwan's ballad 'If It Is You'. It was incredibly brave of Rosé to test herself by singing incognito, but even without knowing who she was many of the panel members still remarked on her beautiful and singular voice. She showed she was funny, too, getting big laughs for her impressions of G-Dragon and Britney Spears, and finished by showing her sensitive side as she became tearful when sending a message to her mother in Australia.

She took part in *King of Masked Singer*, a show where idols perform in disguise. Rosé went under the mystery name of Circus Girl, wearing a mask that resembled a circus tent.

In future appearances on shows such as *Running Man*, *Weekly Idol* and, of course, *Blackpink House*, Rosé's sweet and fun character began to emerge. Blinks learned just how much she loved her food (who else could get so excited about eating toast or green peppers?); that instead of a cat or a puppy she had pet fish (a favourite was named Joo-hwang, Korean for 'orange'); that she was a talented artist; and that Rosé and Lisa were the bicker sisters, forever arguing then making up. On a radio broadcast Rosé admitted, 'Lisa speaks Korean really well, especially during a quarrel. I always lose when we fight.'

Rosé's vocal contributions to Blackpink songs were well appreciated, even acclaimed as among the best in K-pop by some Blinks, and it became customary for commentators to describe her voice as 'unique' and 'what the young people like'. It was in her solo or duet ventures that her distinctive feminine tone, with a reliable range and a thin vibrato, really came to the fore.

Until Blackpink's concert tours gave her a solo spot, such performances were rare and treasured. The first of them came as early as Christmas 2016 at the *SBS Gayo Daejun*, when she sang an exquisite acoustic version of 'Whistle' and joined 10cm, Twice's Jihyo and EXO's Chanyeol to sing Twice's 'TT' – a performance that went viral on YouTube. A month later, Justin Bieber's 'Love Yourself' got the acoustic treatment as Rosé played guitar and duetted with Jisoo on the TV show *Radio Star*. Later in the year, her *Party People* show duet with the CNBlue singer Jung Yong-hwa on 'Officially Missing You', and her performance of Beyoncé's 'Irreplaceable' in front of her idol, Gummy, on the variety show *Fabulous Duo2* confirmed her as a talent with or without the group.

When Blackpink began their In Your Area tour, each of the members was given a solo stage. Rosé took the opportunity to sing a medley of iconic numbers. Sitting at the piano, she sang the Beatles' 'Let It Be' and 'You and I', a K-pop classic by Park Bom, then, getting to her feet, she raised the tempo with Taeyang's 'Only Look at Me'. It was many Blinks' highlight of the show. Occasionally, she would vary her solo stage. At the Melbourne concert at the Rod Laver Arena, Rosé added an extra song, 'Coming Home' (a Diddy Dirty Money song originally sung by Skylar Grey), to her solo stage, saying, 'During my trainee days … I once sang "Coming Home" and … I just started crying [because] I really missed home … so that song has a very special place in my heart.'

It is clear that Rosé just loves her music and she has covered so many songs in her short career, often posting them on Instagram or performing them on V Live. They range from the Ed Sheeran hits 'Shape of You' and 'Thinking Out Loud' to Drake's 'One Dance' and Jessie J's 'Price Tag', and, famously, also include Elvis Presley's 'Can't Help Falling in Love' – shared on Instagram with the caption 'Serenades cause I can't sleep', which gained over 2 million likes.

One fan favourite was Halsey's 'Eyes Closed', which she sang at a concert in Japan in 2018. The US singer was soon following Rosé on Instagram and even wrote, 'You're totally cute' in response to some photos, which elicited a bashful smiley face and a heart emoji in return. In February 2019, Rosé was thanking her fans for their birthday messages on Instagram and delivered a surprise present of her own – a heart-rending studio version of 'Eyes Closed'. She described it as a deep song and went on to say, 'I remember at the time when I recorded it, I was needing some of the healing that this song brings to me.' The song was also posted on YouTube and racked up over 5 million views in just two days.

Since Blackpink's debut, fans have been captivated by her

dance talent, especially as she was selected for the eye-catching backwards floor slide. She took the complex choreography in her stride and during live performances amazed audiences with her ability to sustain even the highest of notes in the midst of an energetic dance routine. Commentators admired the steadiness of her bodyline and the power she found, and many claimed she had the smallest waist in K-pop (and that's saying something!).

The clothes she wears certainly emphasize Rosé's astonishing figure (she is also the tallest of the group). She often performs in tight dresses or crop tops, with Blackpink's stylist saying, 'Rose's style is inspired by the street-mood styling, but with a feminine and cheery touch.' Many Blinks, if pushed, would name the colourful glittery minidress (with that tiny waist cinched in a wide black belt) that she wore on the Japanese debut stage as the most iconic, but there would be plenty of votes for the layered wavy pink iridescent dress she wore on the world tour, the sparkling tank top and silver pleated short skirt that wowed the 2018 MMAs or the two-piece shimmering black outfit that took the breath away from those watching at Coachella.

> She took the complex choreography in her stride and during live performances amazed audiences with her ability to sustain even the highest of notes in the midst of an energetic dance routine.

Off stage, Rosé's style is minimalist and chic, and she goes for minidresses, long-sleeved tops and oversized shirts. She seems to prefer plain rather than patterned clothing and generally wears muted colours with black. The overriding feeling is comfort. Big coats, luxurious sweaters and athleisure are a regular feature of her airport style. In 2019, Rosé even captioned an Instagram featuring photos of her on a flight with the legend 'tracksuitpantsforlife'!

Rosé stans are among the most dedicated of Blinks and even have their own name, Rosénators. On her birthday – which they call 'Rosie Posie Day' – they shower her with love and gifts, which have included a classic Gibson Les Paul electric guitar. She is the most followed Australian woman on Instagram (surpassing Oscar-nominated actress Margot Robbie) and Chinese Rosénators even managed to win the opportunity to put images of Rosé on massive advertising screens in New York's Times Square to celebrate the Mandarin 'I Love You Day'. Rosénators are also very protective of their favourite. In August 2019 they began to complain about how empty her schedule was in comparison to those of the other members, who had lots of modelling assignments and other engagements. Rosé's father even liked one fan's disgruntled posts, perhaps indicating that he too was aware of the issue. As a result, fans took to Twitter and managed to get #StayStrongRosé trending in a gesture of support.

However, the arrival of Blackpink's world tour in the USA provided a huge boost to Rosé's profile. In group interviews she took over as the group leader, proving charming, engaging and supportive of the other members who were not as confident about speaking English. She also struck up a friendship with Ariana Grande. Rosé took to Instagram to thank the American star for her gift of 'the cutest perfume on the planet' and received a 'Love you' and a black heart emoji in return. Now more than ever, the talk was about an impending solo release for Rosé – and YG responded by confirming that the Aussie star is the next member in line for an individual debut.

And there is good reason to be enthused about Rosé's solo and other future activities. She is emerging as one of the stars of K-pop with charisma, style and a voice to savour. She also knows exactly what she wants, as she demonstrated in a 'calm down' message to those becoming impatient waiting for her solo debut. 'I don't know if you guys know me very well, but I want it to be perfect and I want it to be a certain way,' she said. 'There is a right timing for everything and I don't want to rush anything.'

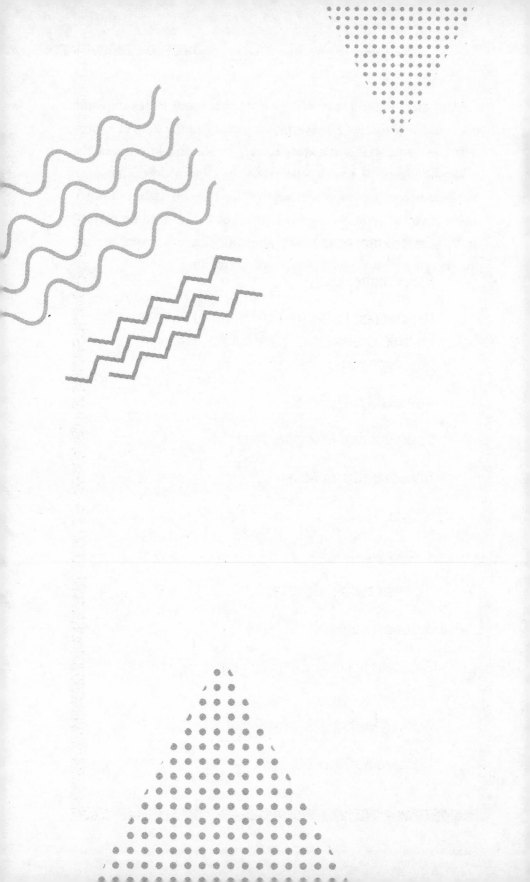

LISA: THE ROYAL MAKNAE

Real name: Lalisa Manoban

Stage name: Lisa

Nicknames: Lalise (or Lalice), Royal Maknae, Pokpak, Queen Lisa, Thai Princess, Elephant Lisa, Flying Lisa

Nationality: Thai

Born: Buriram Province, Thailand

Date of birth: 27 March 1997

Height: 167 cm

Zodiac sign: Aries

Chinese zodiac sign: Ox

Siblings: none

Position: main dancer, lead rapper, sub-vocalist, *maknae*

Trainee period: five years, four months

Instagram: @lalalalisa_m

Lisa is Blackpink's *maknae* – the Korean term used to refer to the youngest person in a group. It is an unavoidable role that carries assumptions, privileges and burdens, even if, like Lisa, they are the youngest by just two months. A group's *maknae* is seen as sweet, innocent and in need of looking after. A certain amount of playfulness and mischievousness is tolerated, but in turn the *maknae* must sometimes act bashful and be willing to ramp up their cute quota with plenty of *aegyo* (displays of adorable voices, expressions or gestures).

Does Lisa fit the *maknae* bill? She can certainly play cute when required and out of all the members she is the best at *aegyo* and has been known to put on a baby voice in order to ask for favours. Blinks have often witnessed her being cheeky and up for teasing the others and her managers, but that is just one side of Lisa. This is also a girl with swag and style, as likely to be sexy and strident as cute and innocent.

Blinks have a special name for her. They call her the Royal Maknae, reasoning that with her dancing, rapping and fun personality she needs no looking after. Lisa herself also prompted another anti-*maknae* name when she asked fans to call her Oppa. Now *oppa* is a form of address used by young Korean women to older men and when some Blinks used it to describe Lisa's 'older brother' relationship with her bandmates, Lisa was keen for it to catch on.

Lisa's birth name is Pranpriya Manoban. The only child of a Thai mother and Swiss step-father (a renowned chef), she was born and raised in north-eastern Thailand before moving to Bangkok, the country's capital. As a young child she was a natural performer, taking singing and dancing lessons and entering competitions. She was part of a dance crew called We Zaa Cool (which also included BamBam of GOT7) and a YouTube clip from 2009 of them in a TV talent competition shows that twelve-year-old Lisa already had considerable dancing talent.

Like many Thai youngsters, Lisa was well acquainted with K-pop; she was a YG fan, and often practised dancing by following the choreography of Big Bang and 2NE1 hits. In 2010 she attended the company's first-ever auditions in Thailand, impressing scouts with her good manners and confident performance. She triumphed in a process that reduced 4,000 hopefuls to just one.

At that point she was known as Lalisa, having supposedly changed her birth name, Pranpriya, on the advice of a fortune teller (it looks as if that was the right move!). Her childhood friends called her 'Pokpak' – Thai for 'princess' – a nickname she still likes; but that childhood world must have seemed so far away in 2011 when, still only fourteen years old, she arrived in Seoul to take her place as the first non-Korean trainee at YG. She knew only 'hello' in Korean, and no one was allowed to speak English to her, so no wonder she was so pleased to meet Rosé, another foreign trainee, in the elevator.

> Lisa credits the other Blackpink members with looking after her and helping her learn to speak Korean.

Lisa credits the other Blackpink members with looking after her and helping her learn to speak Korean. Like all of them she endured a long trainee period with times when it felt that they would never debut, but her drive and ambition, along with the support they gave each other, helped see her through. In turn they would soon discover how fun, caring and talented she was.

The first the public saw of YG's Thai prodigy came in May 2012 when YG posted a video clip titled 'Who's That Girl???' Picked out of a group dance to Chris Brown's 'Turn Up the Music', she was assured, vibrant and clear in her moves. The final caption showed her face – with thick dark hair and heavy bangs – and indicated only that she was sixteen years old, but netizens were quick to fill in the details of exactly who this mystery dancer was.

Lisa appeared looking cool opposite iKON's Bobby in video adverts for YG's fashion line Nonagon, but apart from that it was a long four-year wait until Blackpink's debut. Finally, on 7 June 2016, in a series of teaser photos, she became the second of the four Blackpink members to be officially revealed. She looked young and innocent in most of the photos, but K-pop watchers were quick to point out her fabulous long legs and, among different hair colours, just how amazing she looked as a blonde. When, a month later, the pre-debut dance-practice video was posted on YouTube, the long blonde hair and those legs – along with the fiercest of dance moves – caught everyone's attention.

It did not take long for fans to call Lisa their Dancing Queen. Her performances in music videos and in her solo stage at Blackpink concerts constantly highlighted her talent. And soon industry experts were taking notice, too. After Blackpink's first Japanese show, acclaimed choreographer Honey J praised Lisa for mastering complex choreography in an hour and pulling it off in such a cool and chic manner. Choi Young-joon, now choreographer on hit show *Produce 101*, talked of a private session where he said, 'She is so good that I didn't know if I'm giving a lesson or I'm receiving a lesson,' and top international choreographer Parris Goebel summed it all up by saying, 'Lisa is the kind of dancer who isn't made, but the kind who is naturally blessed.'

At a trainee 'genre challenge' Lisa tried her hand at rapping and loved it. Inspired by Nicki Minaj, she worked hard to develop her own rapping style and, just like she did with Korean, picked it up with ease. Fans were soon delighted to discover that Lisa could rap, too. She was the member putting the black into Blackpink as she spat out lyrics with no little venom. She had the attitude and the vocal dexterity to deliver lines in Korean and English – neither her native language – and in 2018 added Japanese to that list in a version of 'See U Later'. They may not have been her lyrics, but she dished them out with a self-belief, sometimes cheeky, sometimes savage, that made them personal. Songs such as 'Stay' also proved Lisa had a sweet and stable singing voice – something that many fans would appreciate in Blackpink's live concerts.

> Choi Young-joon, now choreographer on hit show *Produce 101*, talked of a private session where he said, 'She is so good that I didn't know if I'm giving a lesson or I'm receiving a lesson.'

It also became apparent that Lisa's on-stage persona was not an act: she was exuberant. On variety shows, true to her *maknae* role, she was the upbeat, giggly, excitable member. She couldn't sit still and just loved to dance. She shocked the hosts of *Weekly Idol* with her instant recall of the choreography to Red Velvet's 'Red Flavor' and Twice's 'What Is Love?' She appeared on *Knowing Bros* demonstrating the taxi dance and the star-pull dance, which were trending in Korea at the time, doing them with such charisma and energy that the clip was soon going viral. And, of course, her version of 'Baby Shark' on *Idol Room* was pure joy.

So TV-friendly was Lisa that she was given her own cable-channel series, called *Lisa TV*. This comprised three twenty-minute episodes in which a camera followed the star's daily life. The mini-series was a treat for Lisa stans, with lots of laughs (especially when Lisa got together with Jisoo) and Lisa, sporting auburn hair, somehow managing to look stunning all day long. However, it was her appearance in the extremely popular reality show *Real Men 300* in autumn 2018 that really endeared Lisa to the Korean public.

Many Blinks were nervous about their idol venturing on to the show, which features celebrities experiencing the tough life of the elite Korean military forces, but they had underestimated Lisa. She was up to the challenge, physically fit and very determined. Of course, she looked adorable in uniform, even without make-up, but she was also utterly charming; being funny – both deliberately and accidentally, especially when her Korean-language skills let her down – and sensitive, welling up with tears when she read a kind letter from Jisoo.

Blackpink is built upon the close relationship of all four members and Lisa is clearly loved by them all. She and Jisoo are like the Extra Sisters, noisy and mad; Jenlisa is a mutually supportive friendship that Blinks adore and despite Lisa enjoying teasing Rosé they are really close friends. Lalise, as they most often call her (although Jisoo has a long list of nicknames for her), also has celebrity friends, especially other Thai K-pop stars, including BamBam from GOT7 (who she has known since childhood), CLC's Sorn and Nichkhun of 2PM.

Despite being based in Seoul and spending most of her teenage years in South Korea, Lisa has always made it clear she is proud to be Thai. Jennie has told how she inspired a love of Thai food in them all and that Lisa has taken them to every good Thai restaurant in Seoul. When the group visit Thailand in *Blackpink House*, Lisa is so thrilled that she becomes a tour guide, ambassador and cheerleader for her homeland. Then in 2019, when floods devastated parts of the country, Lisa made a significant personal donation to the disaster-fund charity.

It was fitting, then, that it was after a concert in Bangkok in January 2019 that Lisa was crowned a Dance Queen. For her solo stage at Blackpink's first performance in her home town, Lisa added a new dance to 'Swalla' by Jason Derulo (and featuring Lisa's favourite, Nicki Minaj). It was a complete *tour de force*, combining incredible energy, stage presence and some outrageous moves. An unofficial video was soon uploaded to Twitter and received 5 million views in days. It was even retweeted by Derulo himself. Six months later, when the group returned to Bangkok for the tour's Encore concert, she surprised everyone with a new choreography for the track. 'Swalla 2.0' repeated the viral success of the original, with many rating it as even better.

With her gorgeous big eyes, small face and luscious lips, Lisa sometimes looks like a living Barbie doll. Even before Blackpink's debut, YG were eager to use her stunning looks for their streetwear brand Nonagon and there was never any doubt she would be a visual asset to the group. And yet Lisa has still surprised with a chameleon-like ability to look fabulous across styles and moods.

Lisa's on-stage image is of the streetwise rapper, and her styling in Blackpink's music videos and stage performances often reflects this with what the group's stylist, Choi Kyung-won, refers to as 'a boyish nuance'. She is often seen in baggy cargo trousers or balloon jeans, chains and bomber jackets, but can also be the member who tries out the outlandish, such as when she matched long neon-green gloves with a sparkling pink two-piece outfit or wore paper clips in her hair.

The feminine touch comes with the cropped tees, sports-bra tops, embellished chokers and dangling earrings. And, of course, in her exquisitely made-up eyes, bright full lips and hair that, although almost always worn with bangs, is sometimes tied-up in top knots and ponytails or extended with braids. Of all the girls, Lisa has changed the colour of her hair the most. Her blonde and light shades have been adorned with pink, yellow, purple, blue, lilac and peach ombrés, highlights, ends and streaks, while at times her hair has also been chestnut brown, strawberry and ash silver.

When Lisa breaks out of tomboy mode she shows she can also carry off sexy, dainty or elegant. As with all the Blackpink members, Blinks have their own favourite Lisa outfits. Often listed among them are the beautiful Pegasus and stars motif tulle dress with see-through slip she wore on the 2017 *Gayo Daejun* red carpet; the incredible rainbow-coloured, lamé fringe jacket that wowed the 6th Gaon Chart Music Awards; or the black and crystal two-piece that slayed Coachella. Most popular of all must be the figure-hugging, red and white polka-dot dress she was photographed wearing at New York Fashion Week in 2018. She looked relaxed, chic and what you'd expect to see in a dictionary if you looked up the word 'pretty'.

Since her debut Lisa has featured in cover shots and photoshoots for the world's leading fashion magazines, from *Harper's Bazaar* and *Vogue* to *Dazed*, and has attended high-profile fashion weeks in Seoul, Paris and New York. In 2019, Hedi Slimane, the new artistic director for designer brand Celine, announced Lisa as the official muse for the brand. Their simple and elegant style suits her perfectly, as she proved on her 2019 visit to the Paris show, when every outfit Lisa wore, from airport to catwalk events, came from their collection.

Off-duty Lisa is altogether different. She has an innate sense of style, whether she is wearing jeans and baggy jackets or high-fashion tops with A-line short skirts. Casual or classic, the vibe is always simple, relaxed and comfy, as typified by her favourite white sneakers, which she will match with almost any outfit. She's not afraid of colour – even bright yellows and greens – but she is never away too long from a stylish black. For this reason, Lisa has become the Queen of Instagram, with over 25 million followers, the most-followed K-pop star on the platform. She is a fashion icon for thousands, including influential figures in the fashion world who watch for ideas and inspiration.

Since Blackpink's debut, fans have observed Lisa's growth in stature – but Blinks know she is so much more than a fashion icon. They follow her to see her having fun with the other members or with her adorable cats, Luca and Leo. She loves her photography (she has at least twenty cameras in her collection) and in August 2019 even launched her own YouTube channel. Called Lili Film, it is a collection of short films shot by Lisa that document life with Blackpink. Rapper, dancer, singer, fashionista, filmmaker … no wonder they call her the Royal Maknae.

TEAM BLACKPINK

When you watch the four Blackpink princesses killing it on stage, it's easy to be entranced by their looks, charisma and talent and forget the work that has been done in the background. As good as these girls are at singing and dancing, they would be the first to admit they would be nowhere without the input of songwriters, choreographers, stylists, dance and vocal coaches, and so many others often dismissed under the umbrella term 'staff'.

One of the three biggest entertainment companies in South Korea, YG Entertainment employs around 350 staff and contracts hundreds more to develop their trainees and support their established acts. These, of course, include administrators, accountants and marketing experts, but also creative talent – singers, dancers, video producers and set designers, many of whom are well-respected and acclaimed in their field. All these people, whose support is vital to the groups they work with, usually prefer to avoid the limelight, their satisfaction coming from the group's success. K-pop fans, though, are an obsessive bunch eager to discover every minute detail of their idols' acts.

To call anyone a 'fifth member' of Blackpink is to ignore the years of training and sheer skill levels of Jennie, Jisoo, Lisa and Rosé. However, it is an epithet sometimes given to Lee Sang-won, better known as Manager Unnie by those following the members on social media. The Korean word *unnie* means 'older sister' and Sang-won seems to play the role to perfection, organizing and looking after the girls but also being a good friend. She is often seen in the background of videos or snaps (sometimes being teased by the girls) and the group have said that the only way they can go out in public in Seoul without being recognized is to venture out with Manager Unnie. Although she is the most visible, other managers do appear in the background of various posts, usually trying to hide while the girls poke fun at them.

In reality, the person closest to being a fifth member would look somewhat out of place on stage with Blackpink. He is a forty-something Korean man named Park Hong-jun but commonly known as Teddy Park. A long-time employee of YG, Teddy is the main writer and producer of all of Blackpink's recordings. The group have said they would like to work with other producers at some point, but recognize that at this time he is perfect for them. Having worked with the girls when they were trainees, he knows their individual and collective strengths and is able to tailor a song to fit their talents.

Born in Seoul, Teddy moved with his family to New York when he was a young boy and then to California, where he attended high school. He became passionate about music and his rapping performances eventually led to an audition with YG and a move back to Seoul in 1998. There he was placed in a four-piece hip-hop group called 1TYM, which became the third-ever group to debut for YG. 1TYM were an immediate success: their debut was one of the best-selling albums of the year and they picked up a Golden Disc Rookie of the Year award. Four more albums followed until military service forced the group to go on hiatus. They never re-formed, but are credited with popularizing hip-hop in Korea and introducing reggae, R&B and other styles into Korean pop.

Teddy stayed with YG but went backroom, producing for some of the company's other acts. Soon he was working with YG's pride and joy, Big Bang, and was trusted with their vocalist Taeyang's first solo endeavours. Teddy had begun to move away from hip-hop towards an electro-pop sound and it was this style that he used to launch 2NE1, YG's new girl group. He was almost solely responsible for the songwriting and production on their debut album, *To Anyone*, and for creating a distinctive electronic dance sound for the group.

By 2011 Teddy was established as the leading producer at YG, working with all their major artists, from G-Dragon to Psy; according to some reports, he even turned down an opportunity to produce for Lady Gaga in order to concentrate on 2NE1. Small wonder, then, that Teddy was given major input into the creation of the next girl group, Blackpink. He was part of the team that developed the eventual four members and would be the senior figure in composing and producing the group's songs.

> Teddy stayed with YG but went backroom, producing for some of the company's other acts. Soon he was working with YG's pride and joy, Big Bang, and was trusted with their vocalist Taeyang's first solo endeavours.

The YG CEO acclaimed his ace producer by saying, 'If Teddy were a designer, Blackpink is the amazing model and brand that he clothes with the newest and trendiest music.' Unafraid to bring in other contributors, such as US songwriter Brian Lee (who has worked with Justin Bieber, Camila Cabello and Selena Gomez),

Korean composer Seo Won-jin and other YG producers, such as R.Tee, Future Bounce and B.I (formerly of iKON), Teddy remains in overall control and is integral to the Blackpink sound.

The girls also had, and continue to have, the attention of top-class vocal coaches to help work on their posture, breathing and technique. Among them is Shin Yoo-mi, a vocal trainer who appeared as a mentor on the TV talent show *Produce 101*. She coached Blackpink for over five years through to their debut and when interviewed on Idol Radio said, 'Every member has strong personalities but if talking [vocal] tone, it would be Rosé. She has a naturally nice voice, while Jennie is good at both singing and rapping, as well as writing lyrics.'

Dance was always going to be a key feature of Blackpink's performances and many hours of their trainee days were given over to dance training – even for Lisa, who was an accomplished dancer when she arrived at YG. Lisa herself is given much of the credit for improving Rosé's dancing skills, but the company employs many dancers and choreographers to work with the girls. In 2019, Lisa even had a private lesson with Choi Young-joon, one of the most renowned choreographers in South Korea.

The dancers at YG are so good that they have reached a level of fame themselves, especially after the company set up its own X Academy in 2018. The male dance team is known as Hi Tech, but it is the female group, known as the Crazy Girls, who have worked extensively with Blackpink. The Crazy Girls are a team of highly skilled dancers who act as teachers, helping the group with the often complex choreography, and as backing dancers in live performances, music videos and TV appearances. They get on extremely well with the Blackpink members and Blinks have become familiar with some of them, especially Mai Murakawa,

Kim Ka-hee, Son Su-bin and Oh Hye-ryeon, as their Instagram posts feature dance practices of Blackpink songs (sometimes revealing the track's original choreography) and snaps and clips of them having fun with the members (particularly Jennie!).

When it came to dance, from the very outset Blackpink showed they were ready to work with the world's best choreographers. In their first official dance-practice video, released prior to their debut in July 2016, they took on award-winning choreographer Parris Goebel's moves for Rihanna's 'Bitch Better Have My Money'. It was an audacious statement of the group's dance prowess and it made many sit up and take notice of these unknowns. It wasn't long before another celebrated choreographer, Kyle Hanagami, was developing original dances for them.

Touted as 'Hollywood's hottest up-and-coming choreographer' by *Dance Spirit* magazine, Hanagami was already a leading name in dance when he joined up with Blackpink for their 2016 debut. His intricate, creative and innovative moves had taken the dance scene of his native Los Angeles by storm. His dances featured on the US TV shows *The X-Factor* and *Sing Your Face Off*, and Jennifer Lopez had chosen him to choreograph her Las Vegas residency. He had also established a reputation in K-pop (mainly working with SM Entertainment) through his work on Girls' Generation and Red Velvet hits.

While working with Blackpink as their major choreographer, Hanagami's reputation has grown and grown. He has worked with huge names in the pop world, including Britney Spears, Nick Jonas, NSYNC and DJ Khaled, and there are over 4 million subscribers to his YouTube channel, where he posts dance performances of his choreographies. His dance video to Ed Sheeran's 'Shape of You' has now reached nearly 200 million views.

Blackpink's association with Kyle Hanagami has spanned their whole career to date, but this does not prevent YG incorporating dance ideas from other experts in the field. In teasing the release of 'Kill This Love' they claimed to have the input of four 'world-class' choreographers. Among them was Kiel Tutin, once the golden boy of New Zealand's world-championship-winning dance crews Sorority and The Royal Family, and now an internationally acclaimed performer, teacher and choreographer. In November 2018, YG posted a 'Lisa X Kiel Tutin Choreography Video', in which the Blackpink star and the choreographer form a duo for a breathtaking dance to DJ Snake's 'Taki Taki' that has now amassed over 15 million views.

Choreography is an integral part of the music videos, but creating a bewitching concept, world or story in just a few minutes is also vital to success. When it came to Blackpink, YG relied upon their in-house director Seo Hyun-seung, who had worked on videos for 2NE1, Big Bang and iKON. His videos are generally full of colour, clever camerawork, bonkers ideas and so many small details that it needs multiple views to take in everything. Hyun-seung's videos for Blackpink have helped them establish a global following, with all their releases being viewed millions and millions of times.

As exciting, amusing or quirky as Seo Hyun-seung's work is, many viewers are concentrating on the girls. What they are dressed in and how they have done their make-up and hair are always prime concerns. Once again, YG don't leave this to chance, employing top stylists to make sure Blackpink's reputation as K-pop's most fashionable group is maintained. Responsibility for this falls to a team led by Choi Kyoung-won, who is also the designer for the luxury handbag brand AVAM (you'll see Blackpink carrying them quite often!).

With some input from the members themselves, she chooses the mix of street style and designer outfits that has become the group's trademark. This involves not only sourcing clothes and jewellery, often from the most high-end of suppliers (some ultra-expensive outfits are borrowed and then returned), but also altering items to fit the super-slender members or to match the intended look. Skirts might be shortened or tightened; sequins and beads are added where necessary; and jewellery is sometimes customized.

Choi Kyoung-won has been credited with changing the whole style concept of girl groups in K-pop. Until Blackpink's debut, girl groups usually performed in identical or matching outfits. It was Kyoung-won who gave each member of Blackpink an individual style while keeping the unity of the group. This impact was recognized in 2017 when she won the Stylist category at the Fashionista Awards and a year later when she was named Stylist of the Year at the Gaon Chart Music Awards.

> With some input from the members themselves, [Choi Kyoung-won] chooses the mix of street style and designer outfits that has become the group's trademark.

For the release of 'Ddu-du Ddu-du', Ji-eun, who had been with YG since their early days, took over as Blackpink's head stylist. Blinks, who watch over their idols' fashion choices with an eagle eye, were sharp to point out perceived changes, but Ji-eun, an accomplished stylist who had worked with Big Bang and iKON and taken the prize at the Gaon Awards the year after Kyoung-won, continued to present the group in cool and elegant outfits.

The Blackpink members' complex, distinctive and spellbinding make-up is an acclaimed characteristic of their music videos. Much of this is down to make-up artist Lee Myung-sun. She began working with Jisoo when she was appearing in a video as a trainee; later, having become friendly with the other members, she became their artist too. Her concepts are developed alongside the girls – the crystal insets in the corners of her eyes for the 'Kill This Love' *Tomb Raider*-inspired look were Jennie's idea, for example – but it is Myung-sun who adapts the look to the individual's features and has the awesome skills and product knowledge to perfectly execute the required effect.

> The Blackpink members' complex, distinctive and spellbinding make-up is an acclaimed characteristic of their music videos. Much of this is down to make-up artist Lee Myung-sun.

As is obvious from their social-media photos, the members of Blackpink have pretty sharp fashion sense themselves and as their career progresses they have had increasing input into their presentation and their music. They have always said how Teddy Park collects their ideas and thoughts for his songs. Rosé is clearly an accomplished musician who might soon contribute to songwriting; Jennie and Jisoo have both shown they can write rap lines or lyrics; while Lisa is known to participate in decision-making for the final choreography.

There are clearly a number of people involved in Team Blackpink. Some of them are high-profile figures, but there are many more whose work goes unmentioned in the press releases and tweets. Each of them performs a vital part of the operation, but when the lights come up on stage the pay-off for all that hard graft relies upon the singing, dancing and visual presentation of just four young women standing on stage.

WHAT'S NEXT FOR BLACKPINK?

On 8 August 2019 Blackpink celebrated their third anniversary. To mark the occasion, they uploaded a YouTube video featuring messages from each of the members and highlights of their career since debut. Two things became apparent: how much they had achieved in such a short time and the affection they held for each other and their fans.

In just nine months, the In Your Area world tour had taken in twenty-three cities across four continents and had seen Blackpink play to over a quarter of a million fans. It had been an amazing time in which their profile had gone sky high all around the globe and, to top it all, they had been nominated in the Best Group category at the 2019 MTV Video Music Awards (VMAs).

The Blackpink fan base now included Shawn Mendes, Rihanna, Ariana Grande, Harry Styles, Ezra Miller, Miley Cyrus, Khalid, Kendall Jenner, Justin Bieber, Little Mix, Pharrell Williams, DJ Snake, Benny Blanco, Drake and Jake Gyllenhaal, with the celebrity list growing by the day. With over 30 million followers, Blackpink had become the most subscribed group on YouTube, while 'Ddu-du Ddu-du' had racked up nearly a billion views, with 'Boombayah', 'As If It's Your Last' and 'Kill This Love' approaching three quarters of a billion.

Meanwhile, the girls carried on working and having fun – although often, happily, the two crossed over. The group went on a summer vacation in Hawaii, which was filmed for a *Summer Diaries* series; keen gamers Lisa and Jisoo appeared in a promotional video for Candy Crush in a dance challenge where they try to copy the animated characters' moves; Jennie cuddled up to Rihanna for a selfie when she attended the Fenty event in Seoul; and the fashion season saw Rosé in Paris for the Saint Laurent show and Jisoo in London for Burberry.

Beyond their scheduled concerts in Japan in the winter of 2019–20, the fourth year of Blackpink is unwritten. Could there be a collaboration with one of the West's biggest stars? Will there be an appearance (and, whisper it, even an acceptance speech) at the Grammy Awards? The promised solo for Rosé will surely materialize soon, but will we have long to wait for the individual releases from the other members? And, as Blinks around the world scrutinize every word for hints of a comeback, will the rumours of a full album from the group prove true?

Could those four young trainees working themselves to exhaustion in the YG dance studios ever have dreamed they would be making headlines from New York to London to Beijing? Their rise has been phenomenal and they continue to

With over 30 million followers, Blackpink had become the most subscribed group on YouTube, while 'Ddu-du Ddu-du' had racked up nearly a billion views.

grow as musicians, dancers and stars in their own right. For Blackpink the sky is the limit. Whatever it holds, the future for Blackpink is bright. Very, very bright.

GLOSSARY

K-pop has its own distinct culture and vocabulary, so you might find some of the vocabulary and concepts unfamiliar. The following is a guide to some of the K-pop words used in the book.

Aegyo A display of cuteness through facial expressions or body language.

All-Kill When a song simultaneously goes to number one in several charts, usually immediately after release.

Bias A personal favourite of a group.

Big Three The three biggest, most successful and dominant entertainment companies in K-pop: YG Entertainment, SM Entertainment and JYP Entertainment.

Bonsang A prize given to up to twelve different acts at an award ceremony (less prestigious than a *daesang*).

Comeback When an artist releases a new single, mini-album or album and promotes it on TV.

Daesang The prestigious 'Grand Prize' at a music awards, presented for artist, song or album of the year.

Debut An act's first performance (usually on TV). The official launch of an act is a crucial opportunity to make an impression on the watching public.

Fandom Short for 'fan domain', it includes everything that goes on in the fan community, from fan clubs to online forums.

Gayo Any kind of pop music.

Girl crush An image that presents women as assertive, confident and fierce.

Hallyu Refers to 'the Korean Wave'; a growing interest in South Korean culture that has spread worldwide in the twenty-first century.

Hiatus When an artist or group are inactive for an extended period of time.

Idol A star performer in K-pop.

Line A word used to link together group members or friends. Often used with a year (e.g. 95-Line) to group individuals born in that year or with a group designation such as 'rap line' or 'vocal line'.

Maknae The youngest member; as such they are allowed to be silly or mischievous and are expected to be cute.

MV Abbreviation for 'music video', usually uploaded on to YouTube.

MR Removed Stands for 'Music Recording Removed', the process by which the instrumental of a song is minimized so that the vocals can be heard more clearly.

Oppa Literally means 'older brother of a female person' but generally used to describe a (slightly) older man.

Rookie A group that has debuted but is still in their first – or sometimes second – year.

Selca A selfie.

Single album Like an EP, with a lead song and one or two other songs.

Solo stage Part of a concert where a member performs a solo song or dance.

Stan A passionate fan. Also used as a verb, as in 'You should stan Lisa.'

Sub-Unit A small group formed from the members of a larger group. It can be a one-off project or an ongoing group.

Teaser Photos, messages and short videos put out before the release of a single, album or a concert.

Trainee A young performer signed to an entertainment company in order to train in dance, singing and other performing arts with a view to becoming an idol.

Unnie An older sister (or sister-type figure) of a female speaker.

Visual The group member who is considered the most beautiful or a member who is included in the group because of their looks.

ACKNOWLEDGEMENTS

The enthusiasm and insight of Blinks around the world as well as the music and performances of Blackpink themselves have been a great inspiration in writing this book. More practical help has come from the book's editor, Becca Wright, whose K-pop knowledge is as invaluable as her editorial input. Thanks also go to Louise Dixon and everyone else at Michael O'Mara Books, Monica Hope for copy-editing and to Lisa Hughes and Nora Besley for their suggestions and encouragement.

PICTURE CREDITS

Page 1: The Chosunilbo JNS / Imazins via Getty Images (both).

Page 2: Visual China Group via Getty Images (top); TopFoto / Alamy Live News (bottom).

Page 3: Visual China Group via Getty Images.

Page 4: Christopher Polk / Shutterstock (top); Rich Fury / Getty Images for Coachella (bottom).

Page 5: Chung-Sung Jun / Getty Images (top); Jordan Strauss / Invision / AP / Shutterstock (bottom).

Page 6: Han-Myung Gu / Getty Images for Mulberry.

Page 7: JTBC PLUS / Imazins via Getty Images.

Page 8: Raymond Hall / GC Images / Getty Images.

Page 9: The Chosunilbo JNS / Imazins via Getty Images.

Page 10: Pascal Le Segretain / Getty Images.

Page 11: Han Myung-Gu / Getty Images for Mulberry.

Page 12: Dimitrios Kambouris / Getty Images for Michael Kors.

Page 13: Neil Mockford / GC Images / Getty Images.

Page 14: Swan Gallet / WWD / Shutterstock.

Page 15: Bertrand Rindoff Petroff / Getty Images.

Page 16: Han Myung-Gu / WireImage / Getty Images.

INDEX

Korean names, unless anglicised, are entered as written without inversion. Thus Choi Kyung-won, not Kyung-won, Choi.

Principal locations for entries are written in **bold**.

Song titles are put in 'inverted commas', albums, magazines, films, TV shows and foreign words in *italics*.